RAND

National Defense Research Institute

IMPACT AID
AND THE
EDUCATION
OF MILITARY
CHILDREN

RICHARD BUDDIN

BRIAN P. GILL

RON W. ZIN

Prepared for the
Office of the Secretary of Defense

Approved for public release; distribution unlimited

The research described in this report was sponsored by the Office of the Secretary of Defense (OSD). The research was conducted in RAND's National Defense Research Institute, a federally funded research and development center supported by the OSD, the Joint Staff, the unified commands, and the defense agencies under Contract DASW01-95-C-0059.

ISBN: 0-8330-2964-9

RAND is a nonprofit institution that helps improve policy and decisionmaking through research and analysis. RAND® is a registered trademark. RAND's publications do not necessarily reflect the opinions or policies of its research sponsors.

Published 2001 by RAND
1700 Main Street, P.O. Box 2138, Santa Monica, CA 90407-2138
1200 South Hayes Street, Arlington, VA 22202-5050
RAND URL: http://www.rand.org/
To order RAND documents or to obtain additional information, contact Distribution Services: Telephone: (310) 451-7002; Fax: (310) 451-6915; Internet: order@rand.org

The federal government provides funding to local school districts to offset a portion of the public school educational expenses of 416,000 children of military parents. This funding is awarded as part of the 50-year-old Impact Aid statute. Historically, lawmakers have been concerned that the presence of military facilities in an area might generate larger enrollments in a community without a corresponding increase in the local tax base. This report examines the workings of the Impact Aid law, especially as it relates to military children. We analyze whether Impact Aid funding is distributed equitably across districts, whether military-related children have comparable educational opportunities to other children, and whether a typical military-related student is more costly to educate than an average student.

This research was sponsored by the Deputy Assistant Secretary of Defense for Military Communities and Family Policy. This research should interest those concerned with military families, the well-being of service members and the attendant implications for recruiting and retention, and the relationship between military and civilian communities.

The research was conducted in the Forces and Resources Policy Center, which is part of RAND's National Defense Research Institute, a federally funded research and development center sponsored by the Office of the Secretary of Defense, the Joint Staff, the unified commands, and the defense agencies.

CONTENTS

Military children living in the United States generally attend a local public school and have a portion of their education expenses paid by the federal government through the Department of Education's Impact Aid program. Currently, Impact Aid provides $900 million per year in subsidies to approximately 1,400 local education agencies (LEAs), which enroll 1.2 million eligible children. Children of military parents constitute 416,000 enrollments and account for 36 percent of program funding.

This report focuses on the workings of the Impact Aid program with a special emphasis on the implications of the statute for military children. The main purpose of the Impact Aid statute is to defray the local share of expenses for educating federally connected students. The assertion is that military and other federal activities bring additional students into an area without proportionately expanding the local tax base.

The analysis examines the sensitivity of program funding to various features of military installations. The funding formula for Impact Aid is complex, and this report provides a detailed examination of how well the formula conforms with the purposes of the statute. Educational resources at military-related LEAs are compared with those for similar districts to assess whether military children have educational opportunities equivalent to children in districts with few or no military children. The study also examines several factors (e.g., student mobility and special education requirements) that may increase or decrease the educational costs of military children compared with those of similar children with parents employed in the civilian sector.

HISTORICAL CONTEXT OF IMPACT AID

Most of the program benefits take the form of a basic support payment derived from two key formulas. The initial basic support payment formula provides a pro rata payment for different types of students. In the formula, the weights for on- and off-base military students are one and one-tenth, respectively. These weights reflect the fact that on-base families live on nontaxable federal land and contribute less to the local tax base than families living off base do. A second, more complicated formula is invoked when the program funding is not sufficient to "fully fund" the program "needs" implied by the basic support formula. This learning opportunity threshold (LOT) formula rations available funding among eligible LEAs based on the federally connected share of students and expenditures in each LEA.

The nature of the Impact Aid program has changed somewhat over its 50-year history. Program spending (in real dollars) grew sharply in the 1960s and 1970s, but funding was cut about 50 percent in the late 1970s and early 1980s. The program has recovered from smaller cuts in the early 1990s, and the level of effort is now comparable to that of the early 1980s. The program was originally intended for military children, but the list of eligible students expanded to include children of federal employees, and, later, children living on Indian lands or in low-rent housing were added to the program.

Trends in school finance have lessened the possible "burden" that military students pose for LEAs. In the early 1950s, local revenues accounted for 57 percent of K–12 expenses, but this share is now only about 45 percent. This reduced reliance on local funding means that the education costs of federally connected students is distributed across a base broader than the local school district and creates less of a burden on individual LEAs. The other fundamental change in school financing has been the movement toward state-level equalization of education finance. Under equalization, the state provides additional funding to an LEA that is unable to raise sufficient funds to meet a state standard. This funding policy also eases funding burdens for districts with military or other federally connected students.

PATTERNS OF MILITARY-RELATED IMPACT AID SPENDING

The LOT funding formula dramatically redirects money compared with the pro rata formula that Impact Aid would use with a fully funded program. The basic support formula assigns weights of 1.25, 1, and 0.1 for children on Indian lands, on-base military children, and off-base military children, respectively. A fully funded program would distribute funds in proportion to the weighted number of federally connected students in the LEA. The program has not been fully funded, however, and the LOT funding formula channels Impact Aid money into districts with high concentrations of federally connected students, especially districts with high concentrations of students with large weights in the funding formula (i.e., children on Indian lands and on-base military children).

This funding approach gives strong priority to funding Indian children and children at isolated military bases with a large concentration of on-base personnel. The LEA reimbursement for the typical Indian child is $3,623 per as compared with $1,378 for an on-base military child. Off-base military children are spread more broadly across school districts, so LEAs receive only $66 per year for the typical off-base child. The LOT formula substantially broadens the range of benefits for different categories of students beyond the range envisioned in the initial weighting scheme.

The LOT formula also creates wide ranges of reimbursements within each group of students. LEA reimbursements for the highest quartile of on-base military students are above $2,275 per year compared with less than $536 for the lowest quartile. Similarly, the payment for an off-base child at the 75th percentile is $128 per year compared with only $36 at the 25th percentile. Impact Aid pays 21 times as much for the typical on-base child as for the typical off-base child— more than twice the nominal rate implied by the program weights for these groups.

As a result of the interaction between the two formulas, the LEA reimbursement for a military student depends on three key features.

- **Number of military children.** About 80 percent of military children are in 116 LEAs with more than 1,000 military students. The other military children are spread across 602 LEAs. Only 13 districts have more than 5,000 military children.

evidence of the extent of the services or magnitude of these charges. Evidence does suggest that migration will not have an adverse affect on the academic performance of military children.

- **Enrollment variability.** Year-to-year enrollment variability is not related to the presence of military children in an LEA.

- **Free/reduced-price school lunch.** The participation rate of military children is *lower* than that for civilian children. Many military children are eligible for the lunch program, but this eligibility reflects the unique military compensation package that provides "free" on-base housing.

- **Above-average students.** Background characteristics of military parents (i.e., high school graduation status and a preponderance of intact husband and wife households) suggest that the children of military members would be above-average students. The test scores of military children in Department of Defense (DoD) schools and in "military-only" public school systems are consistent with this conjecture.

- **Special education.** The share of special education students is much lower for the military students than for nonmilitary students. The Impact Aid allotment for special education students is small and insufficient to offset the LEAs' local costs for these students. Other state and federal programs provide additional funding for special education, however, so the effects of the shortfall are unclear.

CONCLUSIONS

Based on our analysis of the evidence, we conclude the following. First, the variance in payments under Impact Aid is too large. The "needs" for different classes of students may differ, but the funding formula creates huge disparities for the same type of student. Equity and fairness suggest that the program should move toward an approach that substantially reduces the variance in payments.

Second, the linkage of Impact Aid funding to shares of federally connected students in an LEA is inherently flawed, because LEA boundaries are not defined consistently across states. This inconsistency creates funding inequities under the Impact Aid formula. Several states with large military bases have countywide school districts, so the military share of enrollments is small even near large bases. Other states have several LEAs in the same county or city, so a comparable-sized base is associated with a large share of military students in nearby LEAs. These historical and political differences in defining LEAs lead to dramatic funding swings under the LOT formula. The Impact Aid reimbursement for an on-base student in Florida is $625 as compared with $1,970 in Texas, and the funding gap is driven primarily by the difference between county-level districts in Florida and small districts in Texas. The taxpayers of Florida may be able to makeup this shortfall in funding, but the funding policy punishes them unfairly for the way the state defines LEA boundaries.

Third, the evidence indicates that the education opportunities for military and civilian children are moderately comparable. Test scores in military-related LEAs are generally at or above those of other LEAs in their respective states. Similarly, expenditures per pupil and pupil-teacher ratios vary across districts, but these resources are not strained by the presence of on-base military children. On a less positive note, off-base military students impose an additional burden on LEA resources, so military children in LEAs with large numbers of off-base military children face below-average expenditures per pupil and above-average pupil-teacher ratios. The differences may not be large enough to affect achievement, but the evidence suggests that the Impact Aid reimbursement for off-base military children may be too low.

Fourth, the evidence also suggests that some LEA concerns about the extra costs of military children may be misplaced. Military presence does not contribute significantly to year-to-year enrollment variability. Limited evidence implies that military students may be above-average students who might have below-average schooling costs.

Fifth, special education rates are not high for the military population, but special education funding is a problem for LEAs. The funding for federally connected students is inherently linked to the broader issue of federal and state support for special education programs. One possible improvement in the federal program might be to integrate the benefit for federally connected students with the broader federal support for special education. This approach would avoid redundancy in measuring these expenditures and monitoring LEA special education programs.

Finally, migration rates are much higher for military children than for civilian children. DoD should evaluate the cost that this migration imposes on military children and local LEAs. If costs are large, DoD could modify military after-school programs to ease these transitions. For example, local teachers could be hired in the late summer to prepare new military arrivals for their new schools.

ACKNOWLEDGMENTS

We are especially grateful to Gail McGinn, former Principal Director of the Office of the Deputy Assistant Secretary of Defense for Military Communities and Family Policy, for her enthusiasm in initiating this study. Otto Thomas from the same office provided valuable advice and assistance through the course of the project.

Catherine Schagh, the Director of the Impact Aid Program in the Office of Elementary and Secondary Education at the Department of Education, provided useful insights into the workings of the program. Gregg Spencer from the Impact Aid Office was useful in providing access to program data and in explaining the details of calculating program benefits.

John Forkenbrock, Pauline Proulx, Lynn Watkins, and Robert Edmonson from the National Association of Federally Impacted Schools (NAFIS) offered useful insights into how the program affected local school districts. They also provided useful explanations of proposed changes to the Impact Aid law.

Among RAND colleagues, we are indebted to Susan Hosek, the former Director of the Forces and Resources Program, and Susan Everingham, the current director of the program, for their support and encouragement. We are also especially grateful to Sheila Kirby and Cathy Krop who were part of the original working team on the project and provided valuable expertise on education finance issues. Cassandra Guarino and Cathy Krop provided useful comments on an earlier draft of this report.

The views expressed in the study are those of the authors and do not reflect the opinions or policies of DoD, the Department of Education, or NAFIS.

tion of school services. Although military bases may also have economic benefits for their local communities, these tax arguments have been the impetus for federal funding to offset the "burden" imposed by military and other federally connected children.

This report focuses on the workings of the Impact Aid program with a special emphasis on the implications of the statute for military children. The analysis examines the sensitivity of program funding to various features of military installations. The funding formula for Impact Aid is complex, and this report provides a detailed examination of how well the formula conforms with the purposes of the statute. Educational resources at military-related LEAs are compared with those for similar districts to assess whether military children have educational opportunities comparable to children in districts with few or no military children. The study also examines several factors (e.g., student mobility and special education requirements) that may increase the educational costs of military children above those of comparable children with parents employed in the civilian sector.

The study *does not* assess the tax burden that military members may impose on LEAs. The taxing policies of different governmental agencies are complex, and the tax "burden" across jurisdictions is difficult to compare. In some cases, local school taxes may be low, but a bigger share of school expenses may be borne by the state. In addition, a complete accounting of the "burden" of military children on an LEA would need to include an accounting of the economic benefits generated by the military activity in the area (Dardia et al., 1996). These issues are certainly worthy of analysis, but they are beyond the scope of this research.

DATA SOURCES

The report uses data from three primary sources. The Department of Education collects district-level data for LEAs that apply for financial benefits under the Impact Aid program. The department provided data for the 1994–1995 through 1998–1999 school years and includes counts of the number of eligible students by various categories. The Common Core of Data (CCD) maintained by the National Center for Education Statistics (NCES) was used to identify the characteristics of LEAs as well as LEA expenditure data (NCES, 2000). The most recent NCES data on LEA characteristics are for the 1997–1998 school year, but the most current expenditure data are for 1995–1996. Finally, the School District Data Book, also maintained by the NCES, has information on the demographic characteristics of LEAs (NCES, 1995).

HOW THIS REPORT IS ORGANIZED

The report is divided into six chapters. The next chapter examines the purpose and history of the Impact Aid statute as well as the various formulas used to compute benefits. Chapter Three examines how the size, share, and mix of military personnel in an LEA affect Impact Aid funding. Chapter Four compares the education resources available for military children in LEAs with different concentrations of military children as well as LEAs without military children. Chapter Five assesses whether military children impose extra, unique costs on LEAs or whether these children increase local educational scope proportionally. The final chapter ties the results together and offers conclusions.

Chapter Two

PURPOSES, FORMULAS, AND HISTORICAL CONTEXT OF IMPACT AID

THE PURPOSES OF IMPACT AID

The federal Impact Aid statute (Public Law 103-382, sections 8001–8014, codified at 20 U.S.C. sections 7701–7714), first passed in 1950, was originally intended for the sole purpose of providing financial relief to local school districts that were burdened ("impacted") by activities of the federal government. The rapid growth of U.S. military forces during the Korean War caused dramatic increases in the school-age populations of some communities around military bases. Military bases and other federal properties are not subject to local property taxes, which were the major source of revenue for local school districts. Congress concluded that activities on federal property placed an unfair burden on local school districts by bringing in additional children without increasing the local tax base.[1]

Today, compensation to local districts for the expense of educating federally connected children remains the primary purpose of the Impact Aid program.[2] In addition, however, the 1994 reauthorization of the statute notes that the program is also intended "to help [federally connected] children meet challenging state standards."[3] Consistent with this new language, members of Congress who sup-

---

[1]See Senate Report 83-714, 1953, for a discussion of the purpose of the initial Impact Aid statute passed in 1950.

[2]Section 8001. All references to the statute will use the citation from P.L. 103-382, which is the convention among Impact Aid interest groups and policymakers.

[3]Section 8001.

port Impact Aid cite not only the program's importance to impacted school districts, but also its function in promoting the education of military and Indian children.[4] Since 1991, Congress has asked DoD to operate a supplemental Impact Aid program, which is defined as "assistance to local educational agencies that benefit dependents of members of the armed forces and DoD civilian employees."[5] In sum, the purpose of Impact Aid has broadened to address not only compensation for school districts but also educational benefits for federally connected children. This latter purpose is of particular interest to military personnel, who expect the local schools around their assigned posts to be adequately funded.

A SNAPSHOT OF IMPACT AID TODAY

Total funding for Impact Aid in FY 2000 amounts to $937 million. The overwhelming majority of this—$907 million—is administered through the 50-year-old program now operated by the Department of Education. Only $30 million is distributed through the independent "supplemental" Impact Aid program operated by DoD. The DoD supplemental funds are narrowly focused on districts with a high proportion of military children (including DoD civilian children) and districts that have recently seen large enrollment declines as a result of base closures.[6] The larger Department of Education program provides funds to a greater number of districts that have experienced a variety of federal impacts. Federally connected children for whom districts can receive Impact Aid funding include:

- children of military personnel,[7]

---

[4]See, for example, the testimony of Rep. Randy "Duke" Cunningham (R-California) in support of the Impact Aid program before the Early Childhood, Youth, and Families Subcommittee of the House Education Committee, March 17, 1999: "Our military families are sacrificing for America. . . . We need to work to restore hope to our Native American communities. An excellent system of education is a lifeline for these families and their children. And a fair program of Impact Aid is the federal government's clear and convincing responsibility."

[5]P.L. 102-484, section 386 (1992).

[6]A district is eligible for DoD supplemental funds if a minimum of 20 percent of its students are children of active-duty members of the military or children of DoD civilian employees. P.L. 104-106, section 1074; P.L. 102-484, section 386.

[7]This includes a small number of children of foreign military officers.

- children of civilian federal employees,

- children living in low-rent housing,[8] and

- children living on Indian reservations.

In addition, a small portion of Impact Aid funds ($32 million in FY 2000) is dedicated to school districts in which the federal government has acquired property, independently of the number of federally connected children attending the local schools.[9]

Different sections of the Impact Aid statute provide funding through a variety of mechanisms. The largest portion of funding ($737 million in FY 2000) is distributed in the form of a "basic support payment" (BSP) that depends on the numbers and proportions of several categories of federally connected students. Smaller pieces of the funding package are allocated to districts for federally connected special education students ($50 million in FY 2000), for "heavily impacted" districts with an especially high proportion of federally connected students ($72 million), for facilities maintenance ($5 million), for the acquisition of property ($32 million), and for school construction ($10 million).[10]

The Basic Support Payment

The formula for BSP determines the distribution of most of the Impact Aid funding and is worth examining in some detail. A district is eligible for a BSP if the number of federally connected students is at least 400, or at least 3 percent of the district's total average daily

---

[8]In this report, "low-rent housing" refers to federally supported housing whose school-age residents qualify for Impact Aid.

[9]The federal property provision of the law is Section 8002.

[10]Special education funds are distributed under the following formula: On-base military children and children living on reservations are given a weight of 1.0, while off-base military children are given a weight of 0.5. (Children of federal civilians are not counted under this section of the program.) Total funding is distributed to districts in proportion to their weighted numbers of these federally connected special education students. In recent years, allocated funding for this section has been sufficient to provide about $1,000 for on-base children with disabilities and about $500 for off-base children with disabilities. Unlike the BSP, these funds do not go into a district's general revenues; instead, they must be used specifically to provide special education services. Section 8003(d).

attendance (ADA).[11] For eligible districts, the maximum allowable BSP is determined by multiplying the district's local contribution rate (LCR) by the weight-adjusted number of federally connected students in the district (weighted federal student units, or WFSUs). The local contribution rate is intended to be a rough estimate of the educational cost (per pupil) borne by the local district, rather than by state funds or other federal funds. In general, the statute defines LCR as half of either the state or national average per-pupil expenditure, whichever is larger[12]—on the assumption that about half the cost of education is funded through local taxes.[13]

Weight adjustments for the various categories of federally connected students are as follows:

- Children of military parents living on base—1.0

- Children living on Indian reservations—1.25

- Children of federal civilian employees living on federal property—1.0

- Children of military parents living off base—0.1

- Children living in low-rent housing—0.1

- Children of federal civilian employees not living on federal property—0.05

- Other children living on federal property—0.05.

Children in the last two categories (those with 0.05 weights) must meet an additional threshold requirement: They are included in the WFSU calculation only if they constitute at least 1,000 students or 10 percent of the district's ADA. Children in the first two categories (those with 1.0 weight) are given an additional weight of 0.35 if they live in Hawaii or San Diego.[14] Children of military parents include

---

[11]Section 8003(b)(1)(B).

[12]The statute provides two other methods for calculating LCR under certain circumstances, which we will not explore in detail. Section 8003(b)(1)(C).

[13] We will address this assumption later in the chapter.

[14]Although Hawaii and San Diego are not specifically named in the statute, the enrollment requirements of the special provision—Section 8003(a)(2)(C)—ensure that they are the only school districts that qualify. (Hawaii has a single, statewide school

not only children of active-duty U.S. service members, but also children of foreign military officers who are serving in the United States.

A district's WFSU is calculated by counting all federally connected students in each of several categories and multiplying the number of students in each category by the statutorily assigned weight.

The formula for calculating the BSP may be more easily understood through a hypothetical example. Assume that the Jupiter Unified School District (USD) has a total student population of 20,000. These include:

- 2,000 children of military personnel living on base;

- 200 children living on an Indian reservation;

- 100 children of federal civilian employees living on federal property;

- 3,000 children of military personnel living off base;

- 500 children living in low-rent housing; and

- 500 children of federal civilian employees not living on federal property.

Average per-pupil expenditure in Jupiter USD's state is $8,000 per year, which is higher than the national average.

Given these facts, Jupiter USD is eligible for Impact Aid funding because its federally connected enrollment exceeds the statutory minimum of 400 or 3 percent of ADA. The local contribution rate for Jupiter USD is $4,000, half the state average per-pupil expenditure. Jupiter's WFSU total comes to:

- on-base military children times 1.0 plus

- Indian reservation children times 1.25 plus

- federal civilian children on federal property times 1.0 plus

- off-base military children times 0.1 plus

---

district.) We are uncertain whether the special treatment of these districts reflects unique cost factors in these districts or other, political factors.

- low-rent-housing children times 0.1 plus
- if above threshold, other federal civilian children times 0.05

or:

$$(2,000 \times 1.0) + (200 \times 1.25) + (100 \times 1.0) + (3,000 \times 0.1) +$$
$$(500 \times 0.1) + 0 = 2,700$$

Note that the 500 children of federal civilian employees not living on federal property are excluded from the calculation because their numbers are not sufficient to meet the statutory threshold for that category (1,000 or 10 percent of ADA). Jupiter's maximum allowable BSP therefore amounts to $4,000 × 2,700, or $10.8 million.

The "Learning Opportunity Threshold" Modifier

When Congress does not allocate sufficient funding to cover the maximum allowable BSP allotments for all eligible districts, payments are adjusted downward through the use of a learning opportunity threshold (LOT) formula specified in the statute.[15] In practice, the program has not been fully funded since the early 1970s, so the LOT modifier comes into play every year. The purpose of the LOT modifier is to provide a larger proportion of BSP funding to districts that are more heavily affected. The LOT modifier creates a sliding scale that provides a larger proportion of the maximum BSP to districts with a higher proportion of federally connected students. The LOT modifier is calculated as the sum of two percentages: the percentage of the district's total enrollment of federally connected students and the percentage of the district's total budget that would be represented by a full BSP. The LOT modifier is capped at 100 percent (and set equal to 100 percent for districts in which the two percentages add up to more than 100 percent).

Again, consider the hypothetical example of Jupiter USD. Assume that Jupiter USD has a total annual budget of $150 million. Jupiter's LOT modifier would be:

---

[15]Section 8003(b)(2)(B). The LOT formula was established in the 1994 reauthorization of the program.

- proportion of ADA that consists of federally connected students, plus
- proportion of total district funding represented by full BSP

or:

$$\frac{2,000+200+100+3,000+500}{20,000}+\frac{10.8\ million}{150\ million}$$

which comes to .290+.072, or 36.2 percent.[16] In consequence, Jupiter's LOT payment would be 36.2 percent of its maximum BSP allowable, or $3.91 million.

In the next chapter, we will demonstrate at length how the BSP and LOT formulas affect actual payments to different districts, as well as how the funds are divided among the different classifications of federally connected students.

HISTORICAL CHANGES IN THE IMPACT AID PROGRAM

Since its establishment in 1950, the Impact Aid program has seen many changes in its funding level, in the categories of students eligible for funding, and in the formulas used to calculate payments. The program is due for reauthorization this year, as part of the general reauthorization of the Elementary and Secondary Education Act, and further changes are possible. Figure 2.1 shows Impact Aid funding over time, adjusted for inflation and including the funding for the DoD supplemental program, which is a small portion of the total. The supplemental program began in 1991. As the figure demonstrates, total Impact Aid funding rose steadily through the 1950s and 1960s, peaking (in real terms) in the late 1960s and early 1970s. Inflation began to erode the real value of the program's funding in the late 1970s, and budget cuts reduced funding by half (in constant dollars) between 1980 and 1982. Congress restored a small portion of

---

[16]Note that the 500 children of federal employees not living on federal property are excluded from this equation. When calculating the first half of the LOT modifier, the Department of Education excludes children of federal civilian employees who do not live on federal property if those children are not sufficiently numerous to meet the threshold for eligibility (1,000 or 10 percent of ADA) (Gill, 2000a).

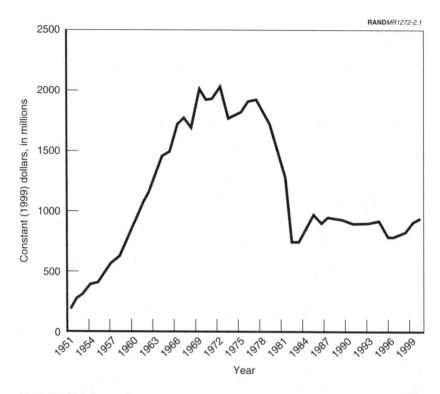

SOURCE: MISA, 2000.

Figure 2.1—Impact Aid Appropriations over Time

the cuts in the mid-1980s, reduced the budget again in the mid-1990s, and over the last five years has gradually increased funding.

The categories of children covered by the Impact Aid program have generally expanded over the years. When the program was established in 1950, the only eligible students were the children of active-duty military service members. After two years of operation, the children of federal civilian employees were added, and Congress extended the program to children living on Indian lands by the late 1950s. Children living in low-rent housing were included in 1976.[17]

_____

[17]For a chronology of the changes in eligibility, see MISA, 2000.

No group of children has ever been removed from eligibility, although children of federal civilians not living on federal property were subjected to an additional eligibility threshold (described on pp. 8–10 above) in 1994.[18]

Over the last decade, the total number of students whose districts are eligible for Impact Aid funding has declined, partly as a result of the new threshold for federal civilians, but also as a result of reductions in the size of the armed forces. As a consequence, the average amount of Impact Aid funding per eligible student has been increasing in recent years.[19]   Figure 2.2 shows changes in the number of eligible students in each major category during the 1990s.

Today, Impact Aid funds go to school districts that enroll (in FY 1999) 420,000 children of military service members, who constitute 32 percent of all Impact Aid eligible students. Military children receive a higher proportion of Impact Aid funds, however, because they constitute 44 percent of the total number of WFSUs under the BSP formula. Of the total number of eligible military children, 156,000 lived on base and 265,000 lived off base in 1999. The proportion of on-base to off-base children remained relatively stable in the 1990s.

Congress occasionally tinkers with the weighting of the various categories of federally connected students. While the historical trend in the classifications of eligible students has been upward, the trend in the weighting of students who do not live on federal property has been downward. In the original statute, off-base children were weighted at 50 percent of the weight of on-base children. This weighting was based on the view that the property taxes that provide local funding for public schools are assessed on both residential and commercial property. The assumption was that property tax collec-

---

[18]In 1994, this threshold was set at a minimum of 2,000 students and 15 percent of a district's total enrollment. See H.R. Conference Report 103-761 (1994). This high threshold effectively excluded many of these students from eligibility in a large number of districts. In 1997, the threshold was lowered to the current level, 1,000 students or 10 percent of district enrollment, making students in many more districts eligible.

[19]On average, total Impact Aid funding per eligible student amounted to $469 in 1995 and $691 in 1999. As we show in later chapters, however, average funding is a misleading measure, because there are wide variations in per-pupil funding across districts.

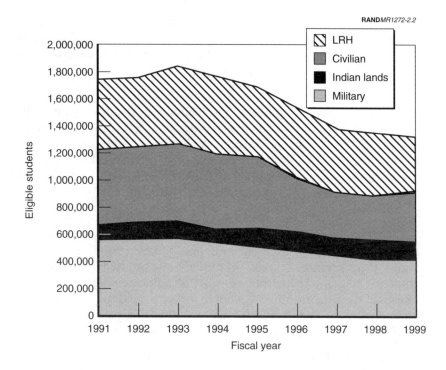

Figure 2.2—Impact Aid Eligible Students, 1991–1999

tions were divided about equally between residences and places of business. Property taxes could be collected on the residences of off-base children, if not the places of employment of their military parents, so the statutory formula reduced their weighting by half. In 1989, after nearly 20 years in which the Impact Aid program was not fully funded, Congress reduced the weight of off-base students from 0.5 to 0.25. Five years later, the nonresident category of federally connected students was reduced in weight again, to 0.1 for military children and 0.05 for children of federal civilian employees (MISA, 2000).

In recent years, the Clinton Administration proposed removing the nonresident students from the program entirely. The Department of Education has argued that a school district that educates a child whose parent is employed on federal property in another district is no worse off than a district that educates a child whose parent is employed by a private firm in another district (U.S. Department of Education, 1995, Chapter 109). The Administration has also often proposed reductions in the program's funding. By contrast, the National Association of Federally Impacted Schools (NAFIS), one of the major pro–Impact Aid lobbying organizations, has proposed an increase in the weight of off-base military students from 0.1 to 0.25. Congress is now considering such a change as part of the program's reauthorization. Congress is also considering a proposal to provide supplemental funding to districts where the military has privatized some of its housing stock. Although newly privatized housing stock is subject to local property taxes, in some cases the taxes produce less revenue than the district had received through the Impact Aid program when the housing was on base. Some members of Congress wish to soften the blow of housing privatization by amending the statute so that children in privatized military housing are treated as on-base children.[20]

The effect of these past and prospective changes in the weighting of different groups of children depends on whether a change in weighting leads to a change in total funding appropriated for the program. If total funding is constant, then changing weights involves a transfer of benefits from some Impact Aid districts to others, depending on their distribution of different categories of children. For some policymakers, however, adjusting the weights goes hand-in-hand with efforts to adjust the program's total funding level. The Clinton Administration's effort to remove off-base children from the program is consistent with a desire to reduce total program funding. By the same token, increasing the weight of off-base students from 0.1 to 0.25 is consistent with a desire to increase program funding, because otherwise the funding of districts with large concentrations of on-base children must be reduced.

As a political matter, Impact Aid is not a partisan issue. Although the Clinton Administration has proposed reductions in funding, the largest cuts in the program's history occurred in the early 1980s, when the Reagan Administration sought to eliminate the program entirely, as part of a broader challenge to federal involvement in K–12

---

[20]See the NAFIS summary of this proposal at NAFIS (2000).

education. Congress generally seeks to protect the program against attacks by the Executive Branch, and a large coalition of congressional supporters of Impact Aid have succeeded in resisting attacks in recent years. According to NAFIS, a growing number of members of Congress have joined Impact Aid Coalitions. The House Impact Aid Coalition, established in 1995, has grown to include 130 members, while the Senate Impact Aid Coalition counts 45 members. Congressional members of the Impact Aid Coalitions divide almost equally between Democrats and Republicans.

As a policy matter, this report examines whether the calculation of payments through the BSP and LOT formulas appropriately reflects the fundamental goals of the Impact Aid program. The extent to which federal activity is a burden to a local community (versus, for example, a stimulus to collateral economic activity) is not obvious in the abstract. In the following chapters, we show how the formulas work in practice, thereby suggesting possible policy guidelines for their improvement. Here it is worth noting that the last half century has seen changes not only in the Impact Aid program but also in the educational finance context within which the program was constructed.

IMPACT AID AND HISTORICAL TRENDS IN SCHOOL FINANCE

One of the most important changes in the financing of public schools over the course of the twentieth century involved a shift in the proportion of K–12 spending financed by local money. Historically, public schools in the United States were funded almost exclusively through local taxes. When the Impact Aid program was established in 1950, however, the nation was in the midst of a long and steady increase in the proportion of education funding provided by state and federal sources and a corresponding decline in the local share of education dollars, as demonstrated in Figure 2.3. The proportion of public school funding derived from local sources dropped from 83 percent in 1930 to 43 percent in 1980, before stabilizing. At the time the program was established, local funds accounted for 57 percent of total K–12 expenditures, compared with 45 percent today. To be sure, these are national figures, which obscure variations across

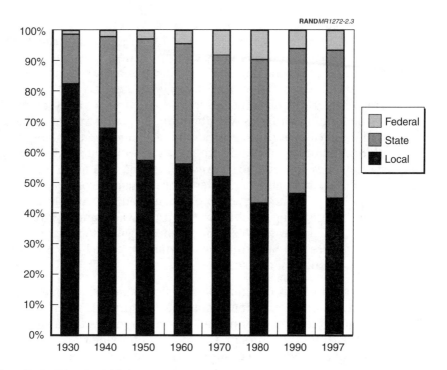

SOURCE: NCES, 1998, Table 39.

Figure 2.3—Proportion of Funding for Public Schools by Source, 1930–1997

states. Nevertheless, this trend suggests the possibility that local school districts may be less financially burdened by federally connected students today than they were in the past.[21]

Although the proportion of all K–12 funding provided by local taxes has stabilized at around 45 percent, in many districts this may overestimate the local financial burden represented by an additional federally connected student. Over the last 30 years, many states have

---

[21]It should be noted, however, that although the proportion of K–12 funding that comes from local sources has declined, the dollar value has increased, even after accounting for inflation. Total per-pupil educational spending has increased rapidly, and the dollar amount funded locally has gone up even as the proportion funded locally has declined. Thus, it might be argued that the local burden of an additional federal student remains substantial.

revamped their educational finance systems to promote more equalized spending across districts. Initially, states subsidized local school districts with flat grants that provided lump-sum payments per student. For the most part, the flat grants have been phased out and have been replaced by funding schemes that provide a much greater level of equity among school districts. The catalyst for reform in the funding formulas was litigation, including the landmark 1971 California case *Serrano v. Priest*, which invalidated the state's system of local financing of public schools as inequitable.[22] In the wake of the *Serrano* decision, the state court systems became the mechanism by which proponents of greater equity sought reform.[23] By 1995, 43 states had their funding schemes challenged, with the state supreme courts overturning 16 of them (Murray, Evans, and Schwab, 1998). As a result of threatened and completed legal action, many state legislatures created new funding schemes intended to create greater equity among school districts.

As a result of this dramatic shift toward state-level equalization in education finance, in many states, if the presence of a substantial number of federally connected students reduces the availability of local revenues per student, the state will provide resources to cover much of the additional cost. State foundation grants guarantee that every student receives at least a minimum level of funding. The grant works in the following way: A state sets a minimum tax rate that a district must charge for it to qualify for state foundation money. If the state guarantees a minimum level of $7,000 per student and the district is able to raise $6,000 per student (applying at least the minimal tax rate), then the state would provide $1,000 per student to the school district. The more the district is able to raise on its own, the less money the state would provide and vice versa. As of 1991, 38 states relied on foundation grants to subsidize local school

---

[22]96 Cal. Rptr. 601. In the 1968 book *Rich Schools, Poor Schools*, Arthur Wise suggested that state higher courts might find state practices in financing to be unconstitutional. Also instrumental in the debate was *Private Wealth and Public Education*, published in 1970, which argued for wealth neutrality in funding education (Coons, Clune, and Sugarman, 1970). These books surely prompted some proponents to seek reform through the court systems.

[23]In 1973, the United States Supreme Court ruled that the federal Constitution could not be used to compel equalization. *San Antonio v. Rodriguez*, 411 U.S. 1. This ruling kept equalization litigants in the state courts.

districts (Evans, Murray, and Schwab, 1996). Under these circumstances, it might be argued that the presence of federally connected students creates an additional cost to the state, but it is not clear why additional federal funds should go to the district.

In fact, the Impact Aid statute includes a provision, added in 1974, that permits an equalized state to recoup some of the federal funding that would otherwise go to a local district.[24] Curiously, however, although most states have moved toward equalization, only three states (Alaska, Kansas, and New Mexico) presently recoup Impact Aid funding through the relevant provision. California, the pioneer in the equalization movement, does not recoup funds under the statute. Although it is possible that many more states could technically qualify as equalized, most states have simply not elected to apply to the Department of Education under the equalization provision. Moreover, many of the member districts of NAFIS want to narrow or abolish the equalization provision to ensure that all Impact Aid funds go directly to local districts, even if those districts are also receiving equalization funding from their states (Gill, 2000b).

SUMMARY

The main purpose of the Impact Aid statute is to defray the local share of expenses for educating federally connected students. The assertion is that military and other federal activities bring additional students into an area without proportionately expanding the local tax base.

The Impact Aid program is administered by the Department of Education and provides $900 million per year in subsidies to approximately 1,400 LEAs, which enroll 1.2 million eligible children. Children of military parents constitute 416,000 enrollments and account for 36 percent of program funding.

Most of the program benefits are in the form of a BSP based on two key formulas. The initial BSP formula provides a pro rata payment for different types of students. In the formula, the weights for on-

---

[24]Section 8009 permits a state that the Department of Education certifies as equalized to reduce the equalization funds that would normally be given to a district if the district is receiving federal Impact Aid funds.

and off-base military students are one and one-tenth, respectively. These weights reflect the fact that on-base families live on non-taxable federal land and contribute less to the local tax base than families living off base.[25] A second, more complicated formula is invoked because the program funding is not sufficient to fully fund the program needs implied by the basic support formula. This second formula rations available funding among eligible LEAs based on the federally connected share of students and expenditures in each LEA.

The nature of the Impact Aid program has changed somewhat over its 50-year history. Program spending (in real dollars) grew sharply in the 1960s and 1970s, but funding was cut about 50 percent in the late 1970s and early 1980s. The program has recovered from smaller cuts in the early 1990s, and the level of effort is now comparable to that in the early 1980s. The program was originally for military children, but the list of eligible students expanded to include children of federal employees, then children living on Indian lands, and finally children living in low-rent housing.

Trends in school finance have lessened the possible "burden" that military students pose for LEAs. In the early 1950s, local revenues accounted for 57 percent of K–12 expenses, but this percentage is now only about 45 percent. This reduced reliance on local funding means that the education costs of federally connected students are spread across a broader base than the local school district. The other fundamental change in school financing has been the movement toward state-level equalization of education finance. Under equalization, the state provides additional funding to an LEA that is unable to raise sufficient funds to meet a state standard. This funding policy also eases funding burdens for districts with military or other federally connected students. In short, it is not clear whether the statute has outlived its original purpose.

---

[25]Off-base members pay property tax on owned residential property or an implicit property tax through rental property. On-base members live on federal property that is not taxable by the local or state government.

Chapter Three

PATTERNS OF MILITARY-RELATED IMPACT AID SPENDING

In the 1998–1999 school year, the federal government provided Impact Aid funding for about 416,000 military-related children in 718 LEAs. The military population was divided into 155,000 students living on base (given a weight of one) and 261,000 students living off base (given a weight of 0.1), so the total number of weighted military students was about 189,000.[1] The total Department of Education payments for military students was $244 million, or about 36 percent of the Impact Aid funding awarded under the BSP program.

The intent of the LOT formula is to distribute funds to LEAs in proportion to local "needs." By design, this approach means that some districts will be reimbursed more than others for providing comparable educational services to students. For example, the Impact Aid reimbursement for an on-base military student will be higher in a district with a high concentration of federally connected students than in a district with few federally connected students.

We will rely on two types of measures to analyze patterns of Impact Aid spending across LEAs. First, we will examine the average payment a district receives for educating a federally connected student. As discussed in Chapter Two, total payments to a district reflect sev-

---

[1] "On-base" housing connotes that the family resides in government-owned housing on government property. In many cases, this property and housing is not necessarily part of the base, per se, and is not separated from the local civilian community by a fence or any other well-defined barrier. "Off-base" housing connotes that the family rents or owns private housing in the civilian community.

eral factors, including the types of federally connected students and their concentration in the district (we discuss these factors in detail later in this chapter). A useful metric for comparing cross-district payments is the ratio of Impact Aid payments in a district relative to weighted federal student units (WFSUs) there. Payments-per-WFSU is useful because it standardizes the student population according to the weights established in the law and allows us to compare whether districts receive different per-student payments for comparable students. In comparing two districts, it is useful to assess whether differences in reimbursement are related to differences in the mix of students (i.e., more off-base children or children in low-rent housing) or different reimbursements for comparable students.

The second measure useful for our analysis is the range of payments for federally connected students. Under the LOT formula, the payment for an on-base military child, for example, will vary from place to place depending on how many other federally connected students are in the district, the size of the district, and other factors from the formula. For each type of student, we will examine the range of payments across districts. The LOT formula ensures that the average payment per WFSU is greater in districts with a large share of federal students (especially if those students have high weights, such as on-base and Indian children) than in districts with a small share of federal students (especially if those students have low weights, such as off-base military and children in low-rent housing). We will examine payment patterns for different classes of students (military versus Indian children) as well as the distribution of payments across districts for a particular class of student.

The LOT formula shifts available funds toward LEAs with high concentrations of military and other federally connected students. This results in large differences between payments for different categories of students and considerable variation around the median payment per WFSU. Figure 3.1 shows the median payment for military, Indian, and other federally connected students in the 1998–1999 school year. The figure also shows the wide range of payments for each category of students.[2,3]

---

[2]In Figure 3.1, the bars represent the median payment for each type of student. The diamond and dot represent the payments at the 75th and 25th percentiles, respec-

The median payment per WFSU for an Indian student is 2.3 and 5.6 times the payment for military and other students, respectively. The LOT formula creates large differences in payment per WFSU because it shifts funds toward LEAs with large concentrations of federally connected students. Indian lands are isolated, so the Indian children are large concentrations in their respective LEAs, and the LOT formula rewards these districts with a large share of the maximum BSP that would be available under a fully funded Impact Aid program. The LOT formula awards the same payment as a fully funded program for 46 percent of Indian children. Some military bases are isolated, but most are near cities, so only 8 percent of military children

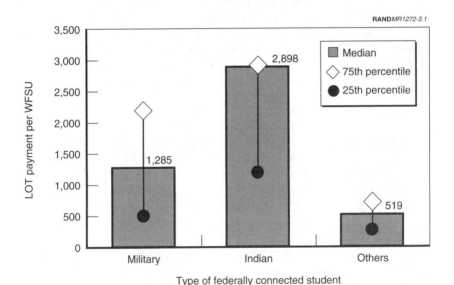

Figure 3.1—LOT Payment per WFSU by Type of Student

tively. The vertical line connecting the diamond and the dot represents the interquartile range of payments.

[3]For Indian students, the payment at the 75th is the same as the median. This occurs because the reimbursement for more than half of the Indian children is $2,898 per year. This figure is half of the national average per-pupil expenditure. Most Indian students reside in states with per-pupil school expenditures below the national average, so the LCR for these districts is the national average per-pupil expenditure.

received the same payments as under a fully funded program. At the opposite extreme, the children of other federally connected parents are generally located in cities where they constitute much smaller shares of enrollment, so their LOT payments are much lower. LEA payments are at the fully funded level for only 4 percent of other federally connected children.

Figure 3.1 also shows the wide variance in LOT payments within each type of federally connected student. In 1998–1999, the LEA reimbursement per WFSU was only $515 at the 25th percentile of covered military students as compared with $2,173 at the 75th percentile.[4] This variance in per student reimbursement has dramatic consequences: LEAs serving the 25 percent of military students in the most concentrated areas receive about 56 percent of the Impact Aid money spent on military students. The range of LOT payments per WFSU is also large for the Indian and other categories. The payments at the 75th percentile for Indian and other student categories are about 2.5 times the payments at the 25th percentile.

The funding pattern described in Figure 3.1 is substantially different from the funding pattern that would occur with full funding of the Impact Aid program. Under full funding, the only variation in funding per WFSU would be from variation in the LCR. The LOT formula is designed to shift toward LEAs with the greatest "need" where "need" is defined as proportional to the share of federally connected students in the district. The premise of the policy is that districts with high concentrations of federal students have limited alternatives for replacing possible shortfalls in local taxes associated with these students. The costs of educating federal students are comparable across LEAs, but the LOT policy assumes that these costs are more easily offset by districts where these students constitute a small share of enrollments.

---

[4]The average district reimbursement per WFSU is not representative of how much Impact Aid money is paid for military-impacted students. Many of the 718 districts have very few military students, and these students are concentrated in LEAs near major military installations. Percentile rankings of military children covered by Impact Aid provide a more representative indication of the typical program reimbursement per military student. The percentile rankings are constructed by ordering the LEAs by LOT payment per WFSU in each district. The 25th percentile moves down the ordered list until one-fourth of all covered military students are included. A similar approach is used to compute the median and the 75th percentile.

This chapter examines patterns in military-related LEA funding under the Impact Aid statute. The BSP and LOT funding formulas are sensitive to three key factors that shape the spending for military students. First, the number of military students in a district is an indication of the possible extra costs that the LEA must bear. Some of these costs may be offset by increased tax revenue or economic activity in the area, but the LEA scope is expanded. Second, the share of military students in an area may have important consequences on the ability of the LEA to absorb the cost of educating military or other federally connected students. If military students are a small share of the students, then the "burden" of educating these students may require only a small increase in local effort or a small reduction in local services. Finally, the mix of on- and off-base military families has key effects on LEA funding. On-base students receive 10 times more weight in the BSP formula than off-base students, and the LOT formula implicitly shifts additional funds away from off-base students toward on-base students. After describing the patterns in the number, share, and mix of military students, the chapter examines the consequences of these variables on large differences in LEA funding per military student.

NUMBER OF MILITARY CHILDREN IN DISTRICT

Military facilities in an area may substantially increase the number of children eligible for local public schools. Extra students mean that the school district must employ extra teachers and staff as well as provide extra facilities. These extra costs are roughly proportional to the number of military children in the district.[5]

Most of the 718 districts receiving military-related Impact Aid funding had very few military children. As Figure 3.2 shows, about 56 percent of the 718 LEAs had fewer than 100 military children. Of the districts receiving Impact Aid funding, 76 percent would not meet the legal criteria of having at least 400 military children. These small

---

[5]Educational costs are generally characterized in terms of "expenditures per pupil." Implicit in this characterization is the assumption that per-pupil costs neither rise nor fall substantially with the number of students in the LEA. Chapter Four will compare expenditures per pupil in LEAs with and without military-related students.

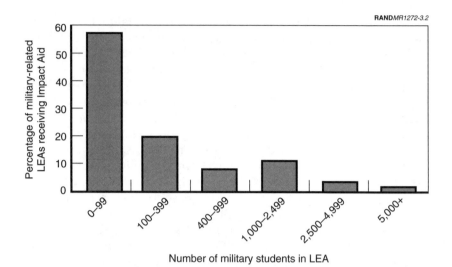

Figure 3.2—Percentage of Military-Related LEAs by Number of Military Children

districts receive Impact Aid funding either because other federally connected children in the district push the number of federally connected students above 400 or because there is a high concentration of federally connected children in the district (the LEA meets the 3 percent share of federally connected students requirement).

What are the characteristics of these districts with fewer than 400 military students? About 40 percent of the LEAs with fewer than 400 military children are within 25 miles of a major military installation, but these districts are not closest to the base or receiving most of the military children from the base. For example, 1,731 children from Tinker AFB (near Oklahoma City, Oklahoma) attend school in the Mid-Del system adjacent to the base, but much smaller numbers of students attend the nearby Moore (801), Choctaw (314), Harrah (61), McLoud (50), and Little Axe (29), and Dale (6) school districts. The other 60 percent of districts with fewer than 400 students are more than 25 miles from a major installation. These military members are primarily military recruiters or full-time military members affiliated with the Reserve Components.

Figure 3.3 shows that districts with fewer than 400 military children constitute less than 10 percent of the military children covered by the Impact Aid law. About 80 percent of military children are in districts with more than 1,000 military students (116 LEAs). These 116 districts are near major military installations.

Table 3.1 shows the LEAs with the largest enrollments of military children. Several large Army, Navy, and Air Force bases are located near Norfolk, Virginia: The students from these military families make up three of the 10 largest contingents of military students in the country. Similarly, large groups of students are located near clusters of bases in Hawaii, northern Virginia, and San Diego. On-base students at Fort Campbell,[6] Camp Lejeune, and Fort Bragg are enrolled in DoD schools, so the Clarksville-Montgomery, Onslow, and Cumberland enrollment figures represent only a portion of the

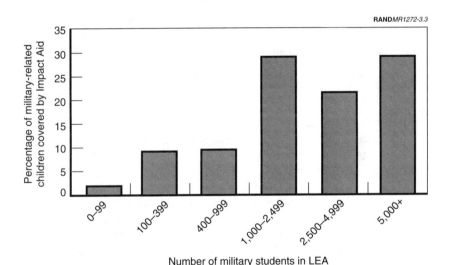

Figure 3.3—Percentage of Military-Related Children Covered by Impact Aid by the Number of Military Children in the LEA

---

[6]Fort Campbell is on the Kentucky and Tennessee border. The base is generally considered to be in Kentucky, but the corresponding off-base housing is in nearby Clarksville and Montgomery County, Tennessee.

Table 3.1

LEAs with More Than 5,000 Military Children

LEA	Base or Bases (State)	Military Enrollment
Virginia Beach City School Board	Various bases in Norfolk area	21,460
Killeen Independent	Fort Hood, Tex.	13,493
Cumberland County Board of Education	Fort Bragg/Pope AFB, N.C.	11,974
San Diego Unified	Navy/Marine Corps bases in San Diego, Calif.	11,855
Central Administrative	Various bases in Hawaii	10,817
Fairfax County Public Schools	Various bases in northern Virginia	10,676
Okaloosa County School Board	Eglin AFB, Fla.	6,902
Norfolk City School Board	Various bases in Norfolk area	6,243
Onslow County Board of Education	Camp Lejeune, N.C.	5,714
Chesapeake City School Board	Various bases in Norfolk area	5,315
Lawton	Fort Sill, Okla.	5,240
Clarksville-Montgomery County Board of Education	Fort Campbell, Ky.	5,116
Alaska State Department of Education	On-base housing in Anchorage/Fairbanks	5,084

military children associated with each base.[7] Alaska has a special arrangement with the Department of Education: The state collects Impact Aid funds for on-base military students in Fairbanks and Anchorage and reimburses Fairbanks–North Star Borough and Anchorage school districts for educating military children in these areas. Two districts on the list (Eglin AFB and Fort Bragg/Pope AFB) contain large bases in areas that define a school district as the entire local county, making the number of students in the district larger than in comparably sized bases served by several school districts.

SHARE OF MILITARY STUDENTS IN DISTRICT

Military students are concentrated in relatively few districts where their numbers are large and their share of LEA enrollments is rela-

---

[7]Pope AFB has a few on-base housing units, but these students attend Cumberland schools.

tively high. Despite the fact that the average military enrollment share across the 718 LEAs receiving Impact Aid is 7.7 percent, most military students are concentrated in a small share of LEAs. As a result, the average military student is in a school district where the enrollment share is 21.6 percent.

Figure 3.4 shows the pattern of enrollment share by different numbers of military enrollments. In general, LEAs with small numbers of military children are also districts with small shares of military students. In these LEAs, the per-student cost of educating military children may be comparable to that in districts with more military students, but the "burden" of educating the military children can be spread across a larger population base. In a few cases, however, even a small number of military students constitute a large enrollment share, because the size of the LEA is small. For example, a few military children from Fort Sill attend schools in nearby Flower Mound and Bishop LEAs, which have small military enrollments of 35 and 79 students, respectively. However, the military enrollments are 25 and

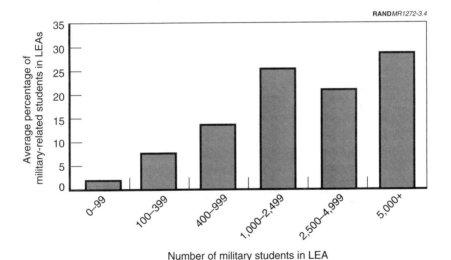

Number of military students in LEA

Figure 3.4—Average Percentage of Military Children in LEA by the Number of Military Children in the LEA

lars, because the LOT formula rewards military share of enrollment. These shares are smaller than they would be if the LEA boundaries were defined more narrowly as portions of the county.

Two large LEAs are dominated by military students. Fort Hood is a large base in a somewhat isolated part of Texas, so the civilian population is small compared with the military population, and 51 percent of students have a parent in the military. Most military members in Alaska live on or around bases in Anchorage and Fairbanks. However, the Alaska Board of Education has created an administrative LEA to include these federally connected students. This administrative arrangement pushes the percentage of military students in this unique LEA to 77 percent,[8] but military students actually constitute only 13 percent of students in Fairbanks and Anchorage.[9]

Table 3.3 lists all 23 LEAs where the majority of students have a military parent. As discussed earlier, the Killeen and Alaska Department of Education LEAs are the only ones with more than 5,000 students and more than a 50 percent share of military enrollments. At the other extreme, about 100 military children from small military facilities attend school in very small districts, where they are a majority of the enrollments. These small, concentrated military enrollments correspond to two Coast Guard training centers in Petaluma, California, and Cape May, New Jersey, as well as a small Navy facility in Winter Harbor, Maine.

Most of the districts in Table 3.3 have 1,000 to 2,500 military students and correspond to moderate- to small-sized installations. The Air Force is prominent in this list of LEAs with military majorities, because their airfields have historically been located in remote locations with few nearby civilians.

---

[8]The Alaska State Department of Education has a student enrollment of 6,624. The "district" has 5,084 children of on-base military personnel, 162 children living on Indian lands, and 1,378 civilians not covered by the Impact Aid statute (i.e., the civilians are not federally connected).

[9]The database does not distinguish between on-base students at Fairbanks and Anchorage, so the text reflects the average percentage of military students across both districts combined.

Table 3.3

LEAs with More Than 50 Percent Military Children

LEA	Base or Bases (State)	Military Enrollment	Percentage of Military Enrollment in LEA
Grand Forks AFB	Grand Forks AFB, N.D.	1,852	100
Minot AFB	Minot AFB, N.D.	1,580	100
Lackland Independent	Lackland AFB, Tex.	828	99
Fort Huachuca Accommodation Schools	Fort Huachuca, Ariz.	1,318	98
Randolph Field Independent	Randolph AFB, Tex.	1,021	98
Fort Sam Houston Independent	Fort Sam Houston, Tex.	1,222	98
Fort Leavenworth Unified	Fort Leavenworth, Kan.	1,596	96
Alaska State Department of Education	On-base military students in Anchorage/Fairbanks	5,084	77
North Hanover Township Board of Education	McGuire AFB, N.J.	1,092	71
Muroc Joint Unified	Edwards AFB, Calif.	1,638	65
Two Rock Union	Petaluma Coast Guard Training Center, Calif.	112	63
Winter Harbor School Department	Winter Harbor Naval Security Group, Me.	86	63
Central Unified	Lemoore NAS, Calif.	1,113	63
Waynesville R-VI	Fort Leonard Wood, Mo.	2,501	60
Silver Valley Unified	Fort Irwin, Calif.	1,570	60
Wheatland	Beale AFB, Calif.	1,057	59
Knob Noster R-VIII	Whiteman AFB, Mo.	1,003	59
Cape May City Board of Education	Cape May Coast Guard Training Center, N.J.	127	56
Mascoutah Comm. Unit	Scott AFB, Ill.	1,527	56
El Paso County	Fort Carson, Peterson AFB, Colo.	2,278	55
Killeen Independent	Fort Hood, Tex.	13,493	51
Douglas	Ellsworth AFB, S.D.	1,190	51
Travis Unified	Travis AFB, Calif.	2,394	51

The seven largest concentrations of military students are at bases where the LEA almost exclusively serves the on-base military community. In part, this concentration reflects the isolation of these bases. On the other hand, the concentration also reflects how district borders are defined. The bases are not so isolated that families are predominantly housed in on-base military quarters. Four of the seven bases provide schooling to students of off-base military personnel. These LEAs may have appropriate reasons for remaining autonomous and separate from nearby, predominantly civilian districts, but these district definitions overstate and distort the prominence of military students in the base community.

For example, Fort Huachuca Accommodation Schools, which is in Sierra Vista, Arizona, enrolls 1,318 military children (mostly from Army personnel housed on the base), while the Sierra Vista Unified School District enrolls 816 military students (mostly from Army personnel housed off base). The share of military children in the Sierra Vista community is 28 percent, but the isolation of most military students in the Fort Huachuca district boosts the proportion to 98 percent.

In another example, the children of Air Force personnel at Minot AFB attend either the Minot AFB or Minot school districts. The Minot AFB district enrolls 1,580 military children from on-base families, which represents 100 percent of district enrollment. The Minot school district has a total enrollment of 5,592 students that includes 243 children from off-base military personnel. In fact, the Minot AFB district is a "nonoperating" district, which was separated from the Minot district to take advantage of higher Impact Aid funding that would result under the statutory formula. The two districts share administrative offices, and the Minot AFB district contracts with the Minot district for teaching services. Military students make up 25 percent of the Minot enrollments, but the districting arrangement makes the concentration of military enrollments seem extreme.

A similar districting arrangement occurs at Grand Forks AFB. The Grand Forks AFB district is responsible for the schooling of 1,852 military students living on the base. The Grand Forks AFB district, like the Minot AFB district, is a nonoperating district that is practically, if not legally, part of the Grand Forks district. The Grand Forks AFB district contracts with the Grand Forks district for services. The Grand Forks district has 7,168 students and includes 258 children of off-base military families. By districting practices, the Grand Forks AFB district has 100 percent military enrollment, but the composition of Grand Forks public schools (combining Grand Forks AFB and Grand Forks districts) is only 23 percent military.

The evidence demonstrates that the military share of enrollments depends on local definitions of school districts as well as the number of military families and the remoteness of the military installation. Historical school district boundaries are dictated by state-specific history, political economy, and tradition (Beadie, 2000). Across the country, school districts have been modified by waves of consolidations in the past 100 years, which have been driven by economic, educational, and political factors. The outcome of this process has not been consistent across states or even within states. In some areas, districts are quite small (townships or small rural areas), and in others they comprise entire counties. Similarly, some cities are spanned by a single large district, and other small towns are served by several different LEAs. Whatever the merits of different approaches for determining the size and scope of an LEA, the result of many different approaches means that LEAs are not consistently defined.

Finally, of course, the LEA boundaries may be influenced by the Impact Aid law itself. The LOT formula rewards districts for having a large share of military students, so the law creates incentives for districts to define themselves narrowly. The statute prohibits specific gerrymandering of districts to enhance benefits, but the rules create strong disincentives to consolidate districts to achieve economic or educational objectives. Consolidation of a base-level district with a nearby district will dramatically reduce Impact Aid funding for the joint district, because the share of military students would decline. Thus, the law discourages districts from consolidating, when a merger might otherwise provide benefits to students and the community.

MIX OF ON-BASE AND OFF-BASE MILITARY FAMILIES

The traditional lore of military housing is that about two-thirds of families live in off-base housing in the local community. This housing is "on the private economy," and members receive a housing allowance to defray the costs of rents or mortgage expenses. The remaining third of the families live in on-base housing. These families receive housing benefits in-kind, i.e., they pay no rent for their quarters and bear the implicit cost of forgone housing allowances available for off-base housing. The value of on-base housing is generally preferred to the allowance, so most bases have long queues of families waiting for on-base housing (Buddin et al., 1999).

The mix of on-base/off-base housing is important for Impact Aid allocations because an off-base student counts as only one-tenth of an on-base student. This weighting adjustment in the BSP formula reflects the belief that off-base families implicitly contribute much more to the local tax base than on-base families who live on federal property.

The Impact Aid data are consistent with the overall view that two-thirds of families live off base: 63 percent of the military children covered under the Impact Aid law live off base in the local community. Figure 3.6 shows that more than 70 percent of military students live off base in districts with fewer than 1,000 students. This reflects the fact that these districts are generally peripheral to major installations, so these families have limited access to base housing. The story is somewhat more complicated, however, since even the share off base is also above average for bases with more than 5,000 military students. The off-base share is only 50 percent for districts with 1,000–2,499 military students.

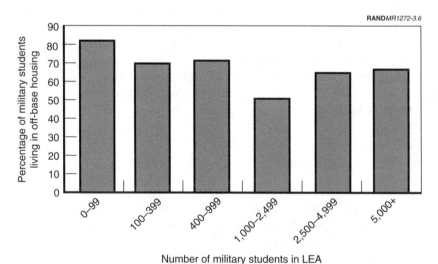

Figure 3.6—Percentage of Military Students Living Off Base by the Number of Military Children in the LEA

Table 3.4 illustrates the broad range of housing mix for many LEAs with large numbers of military students. For example, the Alaska State Board of Education only funds students housed on federal property. The Central Administrative District in Hawaii is predominantly a federally owned area, so most housing is on base. Most of the other districts have very few on-base students. Northern Virginia has a large military population, but few on-base housing units are

Table 3.4

**Percentage of Military Children Living Off Base in LEAs
with More Than 5,000 Military Children**

LEA	Base or Bases (State)	Military Enrollment	Percentage of Military Enrollment in LEA	Percentage of Military Students Off Base
Virginia Beach City School Board	Various bases in Norfolk area	21,460	29	87
Killeen Independent	Fort Hood, Tex.	13,493	51	54
Cumberland County Board of Education	Fort Bragg/Pope AFB, N.C.	11,974	25	94
San Diego Unified	Navy/Marine Corps bases in San Diego, Calif.	11,855	9	36
Central Administrative	Various bases in Hawaii	10,817	33	10
Fairfax County Public Schools	Various bases in northern Virginia	10,676	8	82
Okaloosa County School Board	Eglin AFB, Fla.	6,902	25	66
Norfolk City School Board	Various bases in Norfolk area	6,243	19	75
Onslow County Board of Education	Camp Lejeune, N.C.	5,714	29	95
Chesapeake City School Board	Various bases in Norfolk area	5,315	15	98
Lawton	Fort Sill, Okla.	5,240	31	71
Clarksville-Montgomery County Board of Education	Fort Campbell, Ky.	5,116	24	100
Alaska State Department of Education	On-base housing in Anchorage/Fairbanks	5,084	77	0

available for these members who serve in staff or administrative positions. Most of the Norfolk area students are affiliated with the Navy, and the Navy provides little on-base housing in the area. The Navy has more government housing in San Diego. Fort Campbell, Camp Lejeune, and Fort Bragg/Pope AFB have DoD schools for on-base students, so the military students in the local public schools are almost exclusively from off-base military families.

The LEAs with large military shares of student enrollment are generally in isolated and remote locations. As a result, there has generally not been a large civilian housing stock, and many military families live on the base. Table 3.5 shows that the percentage of military students living off base is substantially below the national average (63 percent) for all LEAs with large concentrations of military students. The only high-concentration base with a majority of military students housed off base is Fort Hood. At 15 of the 23 LEAs, the share of off-base military students is less than 10 percent.

Table 3.5

Percentage of Military Students Living Off Base in LEAs
with More Than 50 Percent Military Children

LEA	Base or Bases (State)	Military Enrollment	Percentage of Military Enrollment in LEA	Percentage of Military Students Off Base
Minot AFB	Minot AFB, N.D.	1,580	100	0
Grand Forks AFB	Grand Forks AFB, N.D.	1,852	100	0
Lackland Independent	Lackland AFB, Tex.	828	99	0
Fort Sam Houston Independent	Fort Sam Houston, Tex.	1,222	98	9
Randolph Field Independent	Randolph AFB, Tex.	1,021	98	0
Fort Huachuca Accommodation Schools	Fort Huachuca, Ariz.	1,318	98	6
Fort Leavenworth Unified	Fort Leavenworth, Kan.	1,596	96	6
Alaska State Department of Education	On-base military students in Anchorage/Fairbanks	5,084	77	0
North Hanover Township Board of Education	McGuire AFB, N.J.	1,092	71	0

Table 3.5—continued

LEA	Base or Bases (State)	Military Enrollment	Percentage of Military Enrollment in LEA	Percentage of Military Students Off Base
Muroc Joint Unified	Edwards AFB, Calif.	1,638	65	7
Winter Harbor School Department	Winter Harbor Naval Security Group, Me.	86	63	18
Two Rock Union	Petaluma Coast Guard Training Center, Calif.	112	63	3
Central Unified	Lemoore NAS, Calif.	1,113	63	0
Silver Valley Unified	Fort Irwin, Calif.	1,570	60	1
Waynesville R-VI	Fort Leonard Wood, Mo.	2,501	60	28
Knob Noster R-VIII	Whiteman AFB, Mo.	1,003	59	23
Wheatland	Beale AFB, Calif.	1,057	59	0
Cape May City Board of Education	Cape May Coast Guard Training Center, N.J.	127	56	0
Mascoutah Comm. Unit	Scott AFB, Ill.	1,527	56	13
El Paso County	Fort Carson, Peterson AFB, Colo.	2,278	55	23
Travis Unified	Travis AFB, Calif.	2,394	51	32
Douglas	Ellsworth AFB, S.D.	1,190	51	11
Killeen Independent	Fort Hood, Tex.	13,493	51	52

IMPACT AID FUNDING OF MILITARY STUDENTS

Impact Aid funding would be simple if LEAs were awarded a pro rata amount per student. The BSP formula does award the district a fixed amount per military student in the districts, with two adjustments. First, the weighting formula makes on-base students worth 10 times as much as off-base students. Second, the amount that the district receives is scaled by the LCR. The terminology here is a bit of a misnomer: the LCR does not represent the "local" (i.e., LEA) level of expenditure per pupil but rather 50 percent of the state or national average level of expenditure per pupil (whichever is higher).

If the Impact Aid formula were fully funded, the funding would be divided by the BSP formula, and little variance would occur in funding per WFSU. About half of military students reside in states with average per pupil expenditures below the national average, so the

LCR is set at $2,898 (half the national average expenditure) per pupil. In other states, the LCR is half of the state average expenditures per pupil. The median BSP per WFSU for military children is $2,898. BSP per WFSU is also $2,898 at the 25th percentile (this is the minimum BSP award per WFSU) and is $3,529 at the 75th percentile. An on-base military student is worth a full WFSU compared with a one-tenth WFSU for a student whose military family resides off base.

The LOT formula is implemented when the program is not fully funded and is intended to "focus available funds on those school districts with the greatest need for assistance" (Goodling, 2000). In fact, the LOT formula takes effect routinely because the program has not been funded to the level of the maximum BSP in many years. The formula rations available funds and reduces median payment per military child to $1,285 per WFSU per year. The range of payments is considerably expanded: The LEA reimbursement per WFSU was only $515 at the 25th percentile of covered military students compared with $2,173 at the 75th percentile.

The rest of this chapter is divided into three parts. The next section develops a simulation model to show the sensitivity of LOT payments to different LEA characteristics. The second examines the patterns of Impact Aid per military students for different types of districts. The final section analyzes the effect of proposed changes in the weight for off-base military students on LEA funding under Impact Aid.

Simulation Model

Consider a hypothetical LEA, Mars USD, that reflects the public school arrangement for a typical military-related child. For simplicity, assume that the only federally connected students in the district are military-related. Assume that the state expenditure per pupil is below the national average, so the LCR for the LEA is $2,898 (50 percent of national expenditure per pupil). The LEA expenditures per pupil are $5,500 per year. Total enrollment is 16,500 students, of whom 2,500 are military-related, and all military children live on base.[10]

---

[10]The simulation is based on the simplified situation in which all federally connected students are military-connected. This approach reflects the focus on military children

Table 3.6 shows the features of the Mars district and how these features translate into Impact Aid payments. All military students receive a weight of one, and BSP per military student is $2,898 (i.e., the LCR). The LOT formula adjusts BSP payments to account for two dimensions of the military effect on the LEA. First, the military share of ADA is 15 percent in this example. Second, the formula computes the ratio of the maximum BSP (MAXBSP) for the LEA relative to total LEA expenditures. In this case, on-base military students have a weight of one, so MAXBSP = WFSU*LCR = 2,500*2,898, and the military-related share of total district expenditures is 0.08 (i.e., about one-half of the share of ADA). The sum of these two formulas—here, 23 percent—is used to compute the share of fully funded payments that the LEA will receive.[11] For this starting situation, the funding shortfall means that the Impact Aid award for Mars USD is $1.7 million under the LOT formula compared with $7.2 million for the fully funded program under the BSP formula.

Table 3.6 shows the sensitivity of district funding to changes in district characteristics used to compute the Impact Aid award. Four cases are considered where another district comparable to Mars differs in a single dimension. Case One describes a district that has twice as many students as Mars, but the same number of military students. Case Two is a district where the military students all reside off base instead of on base at Mars. Case Three is a district with greater per-pupil spending than Mars. Finally, Case Four is a district with a higher LCR than Mars.

Change Military Share. The LOT formula penalizes LEAs with low shares of military-related students. To see why, compare the Impact Aid of Mars with a nearly identical LEA where the ADA is 33,000. Case One in Table 3.6 shows that the BSP formula would award the district with funding identical to Mars, but the LOT adjustment means that this Case One district would receive only half as much funding as Mars. The reason for this difference is that the military

---

in this study. The simulation gets more complicated if various other federally connected students are included, but the basic results are unaltered.

[11]An additional constant allocation formula is applied to this share if the sum of projected payments over all LEAs exceeds BSP funding from Congress. In 1998–1999, this factor was 100 percent, so it does not affect the example.

Table 3.6

Sensitivity of Impact Aid Funding to Funding Factors

Factor	Mars USD	Case One: Higher ADA	Case Two: All Off Base	Case Three: Higher EXPPUP	Case Four: Higher LCR
Local Contribution Rate	2,898	2,898	2,898	2,898	3,500
Total average daily attendance	16,500	33,000	16,500	16,500	16,500
Expenditures per pupil ($)	5,500	5,500	5,500	6,500	5,500
Total Expenditures ($ millions)	90.75	182.5	90.75	107.25	90.75
Number of On-Base Military	2,500	2,500	0	2,500	2,500
Number of Off-Base Military	0	0	2,500	0	0
Weighted Federal Student Units	2,500	2,500	250	2,500	2,500
Maximum BSP ($ millions)	7.245	7.245	0.7245	7.245	8.750
Average BSP ($)	2,898	2,898	2,898	2,898	3,500
Military Share of Enrollment	0.15	0.08	0.15	0.15	0.15
Maximum BSP Share of Total Expenditures	0.08	0.04	0.01	0.07	0.10
LOT Adjustment Factor	0.23	0.12	0.16	0.22	0.25
LOT Payment to LEA ($ millions)	1.676	0.838	0.116	1.587	2.169
Average LOT Payment per WFSU ($)	670	335	462	635	868
Average LOT Payment per military child	670	335	46	635	868

share of both enrollment and expenditures has fallen by 50 percent and this reduces the average LOT payment per WFSU by 50 percent as well. The bigger Case One district and Mars have identical pro rata expenses for schooling military children in their jurisdiction, but Mars has twice as much of those expenses offset by the Impact Aid program.

Change On/Off-Base Mix. Now consider how military housing policy affects Impact Aid funding. The Case Two district in Table 3.6 is identical with Mars, but the military students are all housed off base. Under the BSP formula, the new LEA receives 10 percent as much money as Mars because off-base students have a weight of 0.1 compared with 1.0 for on-base students. The story becomes more complicated under LOT, however. LOT provides an additional penalty for the new LEA. MAXBSP is one-tenth as large in the Case Two district as in Mars, so the military's MAXBSP share of total expenditures is much smaller than in Mars. The LOT adjustment depresses the payments for the Case Two district to only 7 percent of those to Mars.

The Impact Aid law penalizes districts with off-base military students twice—directly through the weighting formula and indirectly through the LOT adjustment. If legislative intent is that military students living off base receive one-tenth of those living on base, then the LOT formula distorts that policy. Alternatively, if the intent is to set the weight at less than one-tenth, this could more directly be accomplished by adjusting the size of the weight.

Change Expenditures/Pupil. The Case Three district spends $6,500 per student compared with $5,500 in Mars. Under the BSP formula, both districts would receive the LCR of $2,898 per military student. With higher LEA expenditures, the ratio of maximum BSP to total expenditures is higher than in Mars (the numerators are the same, but the total expenditures are higher in the Case Three district than in Mars). The Case Three district receives a lower Impact Aid payment under the LOT formula than the Mars district that spends less. The LOT formula discourages districts from raising local education expenditures by reducing the federal subsidy for military students.

Change LCR. Case Four compares Mars with a similar district in another state where the state average expenditure per pupil exceeds the national average. In the Case Four district, the LCR is $3,500 compared with $2,898 in Mars. The higher LCR means that the average BSP for a fully funded program would be much higher for the Case Four district than for Mars. A higher MAXBSP also means that the Case Four district has a larger LOT adjustment factor, so LOT payments are higher in the Case Four district than in Mars. The LOT formula rewards an LEA for being in a state with above-average education expenditures per pupil.

The contrasting effects of a change in LEA expenditures per pupil and in LCR are a puzzling aspect of the Impact Aid statute. The law penalizes districts that raise their expenditures per pupil by reducing their Impact Aid funding. This may reflect the belief that the district is wealthy and can afford to bear a greater share of the educational expenses for military students. On the other hand, the law provides increased Impact Aid funding to LEAs in higher-spending states. This may reflect the belief that more costs should be offset if the level of effort or costs are higher. These approaches seem to be directly at odds with one another.

LEA Funding Patterns for Military Children

The LOT formula produces considerable variability in the funding of a WFSU, and this variability is especially broad for military students covered under the program. The main factor affecting Impact Aid payments is the military share of enrollments in the district.[12] Military share of ADA differs widely across districts, because the military has a wide mix of bases in urban areas and isolated locations and because different local patterns define district boundaries. The off-base share of military enrollments also has an important bearing on district reimbursement because these students receive lower weighting in the BSP formula and because the LOT formula further diminishes the importance of these students for Impact Aid funding.

Figure 3.7 shows the range of LOT payments per WFSU. The overall military payment is further divided into payments for off-base and on-base military children. The figure shows that off-base military children receive substantially lower reimbursement per WFSU than their on-base counterparts do. For an equivalent student weight (i.e., 10 off-base students for one on-base student), the off-base students receive payments that are about 50 percent of those for on-base students. *The actual reimbursement for a typical on-base student is $1,378 compared with only $66 for a typical off-base student.* The ratio of on/off-base reimbursement would be 10 to 1 if the program were fully funded, but the ratio jumps to 21 to 1 under the LOT formula.

---

[12]The share of MAXBSP to the district is affected by the total federal share of ADA and not just the military share. In the case of most military installations, however, the military students in the LEA are the dominant share of the federally connected students in the area. When military members are not assigned to a major installation, they may constitute a much smaller share of FEDADA.

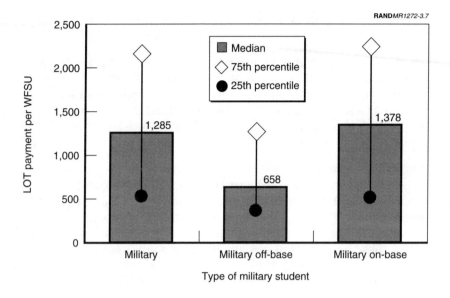

Figure 3.7—LOT Payment per WFSU by Type of Military Student

The reason for the large differences in on/off-base funding per WFSU is the dispersion of these students across LEAs. Although some on-base students live in urban areas, these students are more likely to be located in isolated, remote areas where they constitute a big share of enrollments. Indeed, the military invested in extra government housing in some of these bases specifically because the adjacent civilian communities were small and offered few housing alternatives for military families. The preponderance of off-base housing, on the other hand, tends to be in more urban areas, so the share of military enrollments is much smaller.

The range of payment per WFSU is also very broad, reflecting the wide range in both the shares of military enrollments and in off-base housing. Figure 3.7 shows that the 75th percentile for off-base students is 3.5 times the rate for the 25th percentile.[13] The 75th per-

---

[13]The reimbursement for an off-base military child at the 75th percentile is $128 compared with $36 at the 25th percentile.

centile for on-base students is 4.2 times the rate for the 25th percentile.[14]

Figure 3.8 shows that payment per WFSU varies considerably with the number of military students in the LEA. Districts with small numbers of military students receive disproportionately small shares of Impact Aid funding. LOT payments exceed the national median for military students only in the group with 5,000 or more military students.

The LOT payment per WFSU also varies widely within groups. Table 3.7 shows the payment for LEAs with more than 5,000 military children. The LOT payment exceeds the national median only in Virginia Beach, Killeen, Central Administrative (Hawaii), Norfolk, Lawton, and the Alaska State Department of Education. The key factor in these large reimbursements is the high military share of local

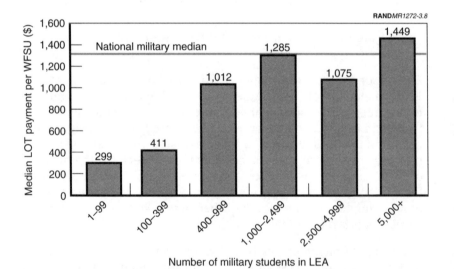

Figure 3.8—Median LOT Payment per WFSU by the Number of Military Children in the LEA

---

[14]The reimbursement for an on-base military child at the 75th percentile is $2,275 compared with $536 at the 25th percentile.

Table 3.7

LOT Payment per WFSU in LEAs with More Than 5,000 Military Children

LEA	Base or Bases (State)	Military Enrollment	Percentage of Military Enrollment in LEA	Percentage of Military Students Off Base	LOT Payment per On-Base Child	LOT Payment per Off-Base Child
Virginia Beach City School Board	Various bases in Norfolk area	21,460	29	87	1,446	145
Killeen Independent	Fort Hood, Tex.	13,493	51	54	2,275	228
Cumberland County Board of Education	Fort Bragg/ Pope AFB, N.C.	11,974	25	94	1,024	102
San Diego Unified	Navy/Marine Corps bases in San Diego, Calif.	11,855	9	36	695	70
Central Administrative	Various bases in Hawaii	10,817	33	10	2,465	247
Fairfax County Public Schools	Various bases in northern Virginia	10,676	8	82	570	57
Okaloosa County School Board	Eglin AFB, Fla.	6,902	25	66	1,282	128
Norfolk City School Board	Various bases in Norfolk area	6,243	19	75	1,449	145
Onslow County Board of Education	Camp Lejeune, N.C.	5,714	29	95	1,173	117
Chesapeake City School Board	Various bases in Norfolk area	5,315	15	98	1,035	104
Lawton	Fort Sill, Okla.	5,240	31	71	1,409	141
Clarksville-Montgomery County Board of Education	Fort Campbell, Ky.	5,116	24	100	1,006	101
Alaska State Department of Education	On-base housing in Anchorage/ Fairbanks	5,084	77	0	3,622	362

enrollments.[15]   San Diego Unified and Fairfax County districts receive only about $550 per on-base equivalent student per year. The Fairfax payment is only about one-third that of Virginia Beach and Norfolk, where the gap is largely driven by the smaller military share in the Fairfax area.[16]   The Chesapeake City schools near Norfolk have a reimbursement rate about twice that of Fairfax and about 40 percent less than the other area LEAs. The irony is that these four Virginia LEAs with identical LCR receive such disparate funding.

The importance of military share for the LOT payment is shown in Figure 3.9. In districts where the military share of enrollment is less than 20 percent, the LOT payment per WFSU is substantially below

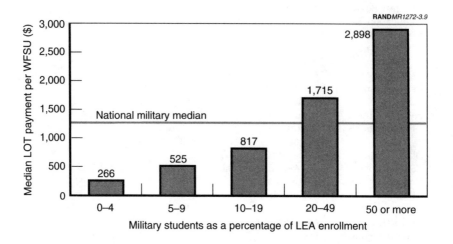

Figure 3.9—Median LOT Payment per WFSU by Military Students as a
Percentage of LEA Enrollment

---

[15]In addition, a few districts benefit from specific exceptions in the statute that boost their BSP formula results. San Diego and Hawaii, for example, are permitted to weight on-base children at 1.35, rather than 1.0.

[16]The children of federal civilian employees are a bigger share of enrollments in the Fairfax area than in Virginia Beach and Norfolk, but the overall federal share is still much larger in the southern Virginia districts than in northern Virginia.

the national median. Under the LOT formula, the military portion of Impact Aid dollars is concentrated on those districts with more than a 20 percent military share of enrollment in the LEA. In districts with more than 50 percent enrollment of military children, the LOT payment is about 2.3 times the national military median payment.

Table 3.8 shows that the LEAs with more than 50 percent military children receive high payments that defray the local cost of educating the military students. These LEAs receive 75 to 100 percent of the

Table 3.8

LOT Payment per WFSU in LEAs with More Than 50 Percent Military Children

LEA	Base or Bases (State)	Military Enrollment	Percentage of Military Enrollment in LEA	Percentage of Military Students Off Base	LOT Payment per On-Base Child
Minot AFB	Minot AFB, N.D.	1,580	100	0	2,898
Grand Forks AFB	Grand Forks AFB, N.D.	1,852	100	0	2,898
Lackland Independent	Lackland AFB, Tex.	828	99	0	2,898
Fort Sam Houston Independent	Fort Sam Houston, Tex.	1,222	98	9	2,898
Randolph Field Independent	Randolph AFB, Tex.	1,021	98	0	2,898
Fort Huachuca Accommodation Schools	Fort Huachuca, Ariz.	1,318	98	6	2,898
Fort Leavenworth Unified	Fort Leavenworth, Kan.	1,596	96	6	2,898
Alaska State Department of Education	On-base military students in Anchorage/ Fairbanks	5,084	77	0	3,622
North Hanover Township Board of Education	McGuire AFB, N.J.	1,092	71	0	5,552
Muroc Joint Unified	Edwards AFB, Calif.	1,638	65	7	2,898

Table 3.8—continued

LEA	Base or Bases (State)	Military Enroll- ment	Percent- age of Military Enroll- ment in LEA	Percent- age of Military Students Off Base	LOT Payment per On- Base Child
Winter Harbor School Department	Winter Harbor Naval Security Group, Me.	86	63	18	2,958
Two Rock Union	Petaluma Coast Guard Training Center, Calif.	112	63	3	2,898
Central Unified	Lemoore NAS, Calif.	1,113	63	0	2,898
Silver Valley Unified	Fort Irwin, Calif.	1,570	60	1	2,898
Waynesville R-VI	Fort Leonard Wood, Mo.	2,501	60	28	2,775
Knob Noster R-VIII	Whiteman AFB, Mo.	1,003	59	23	2,584
Wheatland	Beale AFB, Calif.	1,057	59	0	2,723
Cape May City Board of Education	Cape May Coast Guard Training Center, N.J.	127	56	0	5,552
Mascoutah Comm. Unit	Scott AFB, Ill.	1,527	56	13	3,490
El Paso County	Fort Carson/Peter- son AFB, Colo.	2,278	55	23	2,342
Travis Unified	Travis AFB, Calif.	2,394	51	32	2,167
Douglas	Ellsworth AFB, S.D.	1,190	51	11	2,346
Killeen Independent	Fort Hood, Tex.	13,493	51	52	2,275

funding that they would receive under a fully funded Impact Aid program (the average rate is 88 percent of the fully funded amount). The main variance in payments among these districts is accounted for by differences in the LCR. For example, the highest payments are in Alaska and New Jersey, where the state expenditures per pupil are 1.5 and 1.9 times the national average expenditure per pupil, respectively. In 13 of these 23 districts with a majority of military students, the LOT payment equals the LCR. In 11 of the 13 districts receiving the LCR, the state expenditure per pupil is less than the national average, so the LOT payment exceeds the projected local cost of schooling the military children.

Three examples illustrate the nuances of the LOT funding formula. In many cases, LEAs receive disparate funding to educate similar numbers of military children. District boundaries have a decisive influence on how much Impact Aid funding is available for military students from a base. Finally, the students from some bases live in various LEAs, and the LOT payments for these students can vary substantially.

Similar Numbers of Students, but Very Different Payments. In California, five LEAs have military enrollments of about 325 students. California expenditures per pupil are below the national average, so the LCR for each district is $2,898. If the Impact Aid program were fully funded, the districts would receive identical payments per WFSU of $2,898. Under the LOT formula, Fallbrook Unified High, Lakeside Unified, Lemoore Elementary, Lemoore High, and Los Angeles Unified school districts receive payments of $694, $364, $356, $731, and $17 per WFSU. The formula provides 21 to 43 times more funding for an on-base student at the LEAs other than Los Angeles Unified. The reason for the funding disparity is that Los Angeles Unified has about 685,000 students, so the federal share is about 0.05 percent. From a policy perspective, 325 military students hardly pose as much of a burden on Los Angeles Unified as on the other smaller districts, but it is also evident that $17 per student per year does little to offset the costs of an on-base military student (much less, the $1.70 per year for an off-base student in Los Angeles).

District Boundaries Shape LEA Payments. In several cases, the narrow definition of school districts works to the advantage of local public schools. In Minot, for example, on-base military children are reimbursed at $2,898 each, because they are enrolled in Minot AFB school district, which has 100 percent military enrollment. If the Minot AFB and Minot school districts merged, the Impact Aid payment would fall to $1,139 per student per year, a drop of 61 percent. Impact Aid payments are also $2,898 for on-base students at Grand Forks AFB. If the district merged with the Grand Forks district, the merged district would receive $1,009 for each on-base student, a drop of 65 percent. Finally, Fort Huachuca Accommodation Schools receive $2,898 for on-base students at the Army post. If the district merged with the adjacent schools in the Sierra Vista Unified district, the LOT payment would fall to $1,884, a drop of 35 percent. History, politics, or other factors have given these LEAs favorable treatment under the Impact Aid statute, but equally deserving districts may receive a fraction of comparable funding because their boundaries are less coincident with the military population.

Same Base and Different Payments. In many cases, military personnel live in several school districts in the areas near a major installation. The Impact Aid law provides very disparate funding for these LEAs. For example, Offutt AFB is in Bellevue, Nebraska, and most students attend Bellevue Public Schools (73 percent). Military children constitute 41 percent of enrollments in Bellevue Public Schools, and 69 percent of these enrollments are on base. Bellevue receives $2,191 per WFSU to offset the cost of educating these military children. The other districts do not fare nearly as well under the Impact Aid law because their military students are a smaller share of enrollments and most military enrollments live off base. The Omaha, Papillion, and Plattsmouth school districts receive federal payments of $78, $576, and $427 per WFSU. While the costs of educating the military student are comparable in each district, the federal reimbursement varies widely depending on where a family chooses to live. The LOT formula suggests that the burden is four times larger in Bellevue than Papillion and 28 times larger in Bellevue than Omaha. It is highly unlikely that such wide differentials accurately reflect the true costs of educating military children in the three districts. A reshuffling of students from Bellevue to Omaha would save the federal government huge amounts of funding, while a concentration of students in Bellevue instead of the other districts would draw more federal dollars into the Nebraska schools. The funding formula creates large swings in reimbursement rate, resulting in inequities between adjacent districts serving a single military installation.

Policy Options for Changing the Weight of Off-Base Students

The Clinton Administration and NAFIS have proposed changes in the weight for off-base military students. The Administration has proposed that off-base students would not be eligible for Impact Aid funding (i.e., the off-base weight would change from 0.1 to 0.0). NAFIS has argued that the off-base weight is too low and advocates a weight of 0.25. These policy changes would have three types of effects on Impact Aid. First, new weights would change the cost of fully funding the program. While the law is not fully funded, the policy changes would alter the perceived "need," and funding might be adjusted to reflect this change. Second, the changes would alter the constituencies for the law, because support for Impact Aid in districts with off-base students would be affected by a change in the weights. Third, different weights would shift funds across districts in a somewhat unpredictable manner. The Impact Aid funding formula is complex, and changes in one component of the program would have ripple effects on other components.

We examined the effects that these proposed policy changes would have on Impact Aid payments using the FY 1999 Department of Education data on the Impact Aid program. Our approach focuses on the distributional effect of the changes while holding constant the level of Impact Aid's BSP funding. This naïve assumption is used because the ultimate effect of the changes on funding levels is difficult to predict. The Clinton Administration plan aims to cut the size of the program, but it is unclear whether Congress would cut the program proportionally if the change were enacted. In fact, the congressional budget for the program has exceeded Administration requests for several years. Also, the passage of the NAFIS proposal would not necessarily be tied to an increase in the size of the program that would ensure that no LEA had reduced funding (although NAFIS would like to see an increase in funding to ensure that all districts do at least as well under a modified formula as at present).

The proposed new weights for off-base military students would have a modest effect on the program. The reasons for the small effect relate to the fact that off-base military children are much less concentrated in LEAs than either on-base military children or Indian children. Also, their small weights make them less important than on-base and Indian children for computing the share of LEA expenditures related to federally connected students. Figure 3.10 shows that off-base children constitute 21 percent of students covered by Impact Aid. Weighting diminishes the importance of off-base students as a share of the fully funded BSP budget. The LOT formula further shrinks the off-base share of the budget, so off-base students constitute only 3 percent of the current BSP expenditures.[17]

---

[17]The shares of other federally connected students are compressed even more than those of off-base military students by the funding formula. This happens because

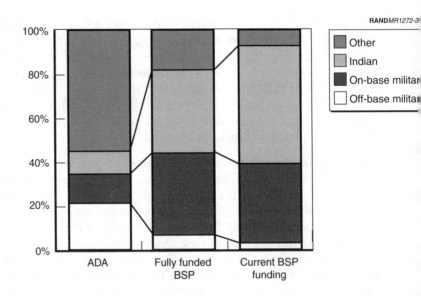

Figure 3.10—Shares of Different Student Groups in the BSP Program

If the off-base military weight were reduced from 0.1 to zero under the Clinton Administration proposal, the military share of the budget would fall from 39 percent to 33 percent. Figure 3.11 shows that districts with Indian children would get an increased share of the budget under this policy. A somewhat counterintuitive result is that the budget share for on-base students would fall from 35 percent now to 33 percent under the new policy. The lower weights mean that off-base military students are eliminated from the Impact Aid program, and this affects reimbursement of on-base students in two ways. First, the average LOT payment per WFSU rises because the total budget is applied to a smaller number of students, i.e., the total number of students covered under Impact Aid is reduced by 261,000 off-base military students. This result would allow the LEAs with on-base military children to recoup some of the money that had been funding off-base children. The second and conflicting effect of the

---

many of these students are the children of federal civilian employees and receive a weight of only 0.05.

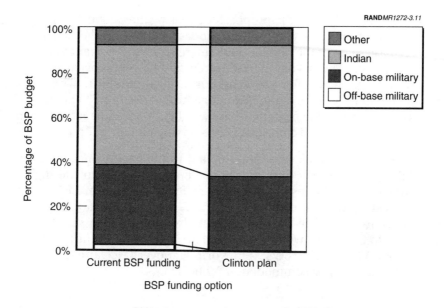

Figure 3.11—Shares of Different Student Groups for Alternative BSP
Funding Options (Current Versus Clinton Plan)

policy is a reduction in the military share for districts with a mixture
of off-base and on-base students. This reduces the concentration of
military students in LEAs and tends to diminish the overall share of
budget funds spent on military on-base children.

The overall change in LEA funding as a share of total expenditures is
small under the Clinton plan. Assuming that the districts are unable
to replace the lost funds from off-base students, LEA expenditure
would change by less than one percentage point in 91 percent of the
districts with military children. The largest loss of revenue would
occur at Fort Hood, where the Killeen revenue would fall by 5 percent. Revenue gains of 5 to 7 percent would occur at Fort Leavenworth Independent, Minot AFB, Grand Forks AFB, North Hanover
(McGuire AFB), and Fort Huachuca Accommodation Schools LEAs.
The gains are somewhat larger for LEAs with Indian children, but the
average gain in LEA revenue for these districts is only 3 percent.

The effects of the NAFIS proposal (increasing the weight for off-base students from 0.1 to 0.25) are also modest. Figure 3.12 shows that the off-base share of the budget would increase from 3 percent to nearly 8 percent. The on-base share would fall, however, because LEAs would receive smaller payments for on-base students. The combined military share of the BSP budget would rise from 38 percent to 42 percent with the higher off-base weights. Most of the reduction in budget share would come from LEAs serving Indian children.

The NAFIS plan (like the Clinton plan) would have a small effect on LEA expenditures. The change in LEA revenues from the higher weight would be less than 1 percent for 96 percent of LEAs. The biggest changes in revenue are for a few districts with a very high concentration of on-base military children. Revenue losses of 2 percent to 3 percent would occur at Fort Leavenworth Independent, Minot AFB, Grand Forks AFB, North Hanover (McGuire AFB), and Fort Huachuca Accommodation Schools LEAs.

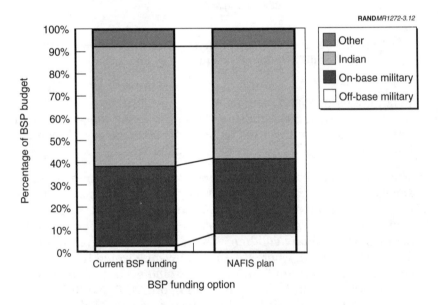

Figure 3.12—Shares of Different Student Groups for Alternative BSP Funding Options (Current Versus NAFIS Plan)

SUMMARY

The LOT funding formula dramatically redirects money as compared with the pro rata formula that Impact Aid would use with a fully funded program. The basic support formula provides weights of 1.25, 1, and 0.1 for children on Indian lands, on-base military children, and off-base military children, respectively. A fully funded program would distribute funds in proportion to the number of federally connected students in the LEA. The program has not been fully funded, however, and the LOT funding formula channels Impact Aid money into districts with high concentrations of federally connected students, especially districts with high concentrations of students with large weights in the funding formula (i.e., children on Indian lands and on-base military children).

This funding approach gives strong priority to funding Indian children and children at isolated military bases with a large concentration of on-base personnel. The LEA reimbursement for the typical Indian child is $3,623 per year compared with $1,378 for an on-base military child. Off-base military children are spread more broadly across school districts, so LEAs receive only $66 per year for the typical off-base child. The LOT formula substantially broadens the range of benefits for different categories of students beyond the range envisioned in the initial weighting scheme.

The LOT formula also creates wide ranges of reimbursements within each group of students. LEA reimbursements for the highest quartile of on-base military students exceed $2,275 per year compared with less than $536 for the lowest quartile. Similarly, the payment for an off-base child at the 75th percentile is $128 per year compared with only $36 at the 25th percentile. Impact Aid pays 21 times as much for the typical on-base child as it does for the typical off-base child. This is more than twice the nominal rate implied by the program weights for these groups.

Three key features of an LEA affect the Impact Aid payment for military students.

- **Number of military children.** About 80 percent of military children are in 116 LEAs with more than 1,000 military students. The other military children are spread across 602 LEAs. Only 13 districts have more than 5,000 military children.

- **Share of military students.** Military members are concentrated in a few districts, so their enrollment shares are high. The average military student is in an LEA where the enrollment share is 21.6 percent. The military share of enrollments exceeds 50 percent for only 23 districts, however, and most of these districts have fewer than 2,000 military enrollments.

- **Mix of on-base and off-base military families.** About 63 percent of military children live off base. These off-base children receive a much lower weight in computing Impact Aid benefits. LEAs with small and large numbers of military children have a disproportionate share of off-base housing. The smallest share of military housing occurs in LEAs with 1,000 to 2,500 students. These LEAs are adjacent to small, isolated military installations where the concentration of military students is high.

Under the LOT formula, LEA funding is very sensitive to the number, share, and distribution of military children as well as to LEA expenditures.

- LOT penalizes LEAs with low shares of military-related students.

- The program penalizes off-base students directly through the weighting formula and indirectly through the LOT adjustment.

- LOT payments are inversely related to LEA expenditures, so LEAs are discouraged from raising local education expenditures.

- The program awards higher payments for LEAs in states with above-average expenditures.

These adjustments are designed to ration available funds according to district "needs."

LEA boundaries are not defined consistently across states, and this inconsistency creates funding inequities under the Impact Aid funding formula. Several states with large military bases have countywide school districts, so the military share of enrollments is small even near large bases. Other states have several LEAs in the same country or city, so a comparable-sized base is associated with a large share of military students in nearby LEAs. These historical and political differences in defining LEAs lead to dramatic funding swings under the LOT formula.

Chapter Four

COMPARISONS OF MILITARY-RELATED AND CIVILIAN SCHOOL DISTRICTS

A key issue for military parents is how the learning opportunities available to their children compare to those for other children. A military base may strain local resources for funding schools, because local taxpayers may be unwilling or unable to pay extra taxes to educate the military children. The goal of Impact Aid is to defray the costs of these military children and to ensure that federally connected LEAs are not forced to diminish the scope of their educational services. If Impact Aid funding is sufficient to provide military-impacted districts with a fair access to funding resources, then these districts should be able to provide educational services comparable to other districts with few or no military children. This chapter compares resource decisions by LEAs with and without military children and assesses whether military-impacted districts are resource poor. The resource measures are LEA expenditures per pupil and the pupil-teacher ratio in the district. The chapter also examines the quality of schooling available in military-related districts and other districts in the same area. An important policy issue is whether military children have access to high-quality schools. The analysis compares districtwide test scores in areas near a military installation with scores in other parts of the same state.

The chapter provides insights into interdistrict patterns of resource use and test scores, but it does not address potentially important intradistrict differences. Education researchers have acknowledged that resources may not be spread evenly within LEAs, but there is little measurement of these differences (Goldhaber and Brewer, 1997). For example, some schools in a district may have a higher pupil-teacher ratio or greater expenditure per pupil than others. If resource use or test scores vary widely within a district, the district average may be a poor summary of the district's performance.[1]

The Impact Aid and Common Core expenditure data are LEA level and do not disaggregate schools within the districts. In particular, the data do not distinguish military-related enrollments at schools within an LEA or expenditures at particular schools. Given these data limitations, we focus here on districtwide comparisons and leave the issue of within-district patterns for future analysis with more refined data.

The remainder of the chapter is divided into two parts. The first examines how the share of military children in an LEA affects district expenditures per pupil and the pupil-teacher ratio. The second examines patterns of student achievement (test scores) in six states with high numbers of military enrollments.

COMPARISON OF MILITARY AND NONMILITARY LEAs' PUPIL-TEACHER RATIOS AND EXPENDITURES PER PUPIL

Parents, educators, and policymakers are very sensitive to the performance of our public schools. For decades, educators have argued for increased expenditures as a mechanism to improve quality.[2]

---

[1]Ideally, expenditures per pupil and pupil-teacher ratio would be measured at the level of the individual pupil. This type of data would avoid problems of aggregating across classrooms and schools within a district. Individual data are seldom available, however, and this study relies on the aggregated data.

[2]An often-cited article, Hanushek (1986) reviewed the existing literature and suggested that no systematic evidence has been found tying school inputs or expenditures to student achievement. However, recent research has provided greater support that a positive relationship exists. For instance, Ferguson (1991), along with Ehrenberg and Brewer (1995), reported that teacher ability has a positive effect on academic achievement. Further, Sander (1993) reported that an increase in pupil-teacher ratios reduces both graduation rates and the percentage of college-bound students. Similarly, Card and Krueger (1992) found that decreases in pupil-teacher ratios have a significant effect on the economic returns to education, and, most recently, Krueger and Whitmore (2000) suggested that smaller class sizes can have long-term effects. Despite these recent findings, researchers still have difficulty consistently discerning a strong relationship between expenditure (or specific educational inputs) and student achievement. This does not mean, however, that researchers, including Hanushek, believe that the total amount of expenditures and inputs have no impact on student achievement. It only means that changes in expenditures or inputs, at the margin, are

More recently, policymakers across the nation and in individual states have pushed for smaller classes as a specific mechanism for improving quality. Therefore, this part of the analysis examines how the presence of military children affects LEA expenditures per pupil and pupil-teacher ratios. These measures are generally regarded as proxies for school quality. While debate has arisen whether marginal changes in expenditures and smaller class sizes have a positive impact on student achievement, it is a reasonable assumption that parents perceive these as signals of higher quality in education.[3]

This analysis expands on existing econometric models employed by Porterba (1997) and Ladd and Murray (2000) to examine LEA resourcing decisions. These public finance models are generally demand-driven and intended to explain variations in expenditures per pupil across LEAs.[4] In other words, they examine the relationship between variations in expenditures per pupil and general characteristics of the LEAs that may affect educational support.

The analysis examines the relationship between a number of LEA characteristics, including the share of military students, and school quality as measured by expenditures per pupil and pupil-teacher ratios. A national database was constructed from 1994–1995 and 1995–1996 school year data gathered from the Census Bureau, Common Core, and the School District Data Book. As part of the process of cleaning the data, certain LEAs were either eliminated from the data set or dropped out during the merge of the 1994–1995 school year data to the 1995–1996 school year data. LEAs were often eliminated because of the unique features of the school districts. For instance, 100 percent, or nearly 100 percent, of special education LEAs as well as county juvenile detention LEAs were eliminated because of the unique students they serve.

---

not having an impact or that researchers have not been able to find the strong relationship consistently for a variety of technical reasons.

[3]Class size and pupil-teacher ratios are not the same thing. Ideally, class size should be measured at the individual classroom level. For example, we would like to know whether fourth graders do better in a class of 18 students than in a class of 25. Pupil-teacher ratio is measured across a school or school district. The pupil-teacher ratio for an LEA is the number of students in the district (or school) divided by the number of full-time equivalent teachers. This averaging masks the differences in class size within district.

[4]Poterba's data are at the state level rather than the LEA level.

In other cases, certain LEAs dropped out because they were not represented in both years of data. For instance, some LEAs may have consolidated over the two-year time frame and, therefore, lack the consistency to be included in the data set. However, the data, even with the cleaning process, are very representative of students and districts nationwide. In total, more than 96 percent of all students and more than 90 percent of all LEAs are represented in the data. This panel database was used to examine both variations in resource patterns across LEAs at a point in time and within an LEA over time. This comprehensive database provides robust information about factors affecting LEA resource decisions.

The demand model estimates how the share of military children in an LEA affects the expenditure per pupil and pupil-teacher ratio, while holding constant or adjusting for other characteristics of the LEA. LEA decisions are affected by a variety of socioeconomic characteristics (e.g., education and income levels in the LEA), other funding resources (e.g., state and federal aid), and local cost factors (e.g., the percentage of special education students, type of LEA). These types of factors are included in the model along with the share of military students in the district. The model also adjusts for unobservable differences across school districts and across time by using a technique referred to as "state and time fixed effects." The state-level fixed effects can help control for differences in state policies, including differences in funding schemes or statewide reforms, whereas the time fixed effect controls for changes over time. Additionally, each LEA observation is weighted by student enrollment, so the results are representative of the typical student. This weighting procedure ensures that small LEAs that educate a small minority of students do not dominate the estimates.

A complete list of the variables, along with the weighted mean and standard deviations, is provided in Table 4.1. The table is segmented into the three vectors of variables and highlights the differences between LEAs with less than 3 percent military students and more than 3 percent military students. As the table suggests, military-related LEAs generally spend less per pupil[5] and have larger pupil-

---

[5]The expenditures-per-pupil variable is current expenditures and does not include capital costs.

teacher ratios.[6] Also noteworthy is the fact that military LEAs have fewer owner-occupied homes, a smaller elderly and poor population, and are generally located in suburban areas. On the flip side, military-related LEAs tend to have higher family incomes and a higher proportion of African-American, Hispanic, and school-age population. In terms of variables that may affect the cost of educating students, the military LEAs are much smaller and have fewer students who speak English poorly[7] but slightly more special education students.[8]

The inclusion of each of the variables (listed in Table 4.1) into the two models is based on an existing literature and reasonable intuition. For example, while Poterba (1997) and Ladd and Murray (2000) included many of the same demographic factors and one of our outside revenue sources (federal aid)[9] in their models, they did not include our cost factors. More specifically, Poterba, along with Ladd and Murray, explain the variation in expenditures per pupil as a function of the district's wealth (median/per-capita income and percentage of population below the poverty line), educational preferences of families (percentage of families with college education), racial composition of adults and students (percentage nonwhite total population and percentage of nonwhite school-age population), the age distribution of the population (percentage of senior population and percentage school-age population), regional characteristics (urban versus rural), outside support (federal aid), and a proxy for after tax price of education spending (percentage of owner-occupied housing).[10] Based on reasonable intuition and the inclusion of

---

[6]The pupil-teacher ratio is calculated as the total number of students divided by the total number of teachers, including special education teachers.

[7]Persons over five years old who responded to a question from the Census Bureau about English-speaking ability. They indicated whether they spoke English "Very Well," "Well," "Not Well," or "Not at All."

[8]Special education rates are higher in districts with military children than in those without, but this result does not reflect above-average rates of special education by military children. Special education is discussed in more detail in Chapter Five.

[9]The model also includes state support.

[10]The percentage of owner-occupied housing can have a number of effects. Poterba (1997) argued that because local and state taxes, including the property taxes of owning a home, can be deducted from federal taxes, owners of homes may have a greater

Table 4.1

Variable Means and Standard Deviations for LEAs with Less Than 3 Percent Military Students and LEAs with More Than 3 Percent Military Students

Variable	Less Than 3 Percent Military Students		More Than 3 Percent Military Students	
	Mean	Standard Deviation	Mean	Standard Deviation
Measures of Quality				
Expenditures per Pupil	$5,630	$1,654	$5,014	$1,030
Pupil-Teacher Ratio	18.38	4.14	19.02	3.15
Other Sources of District Revenue				
Federal Revenue per Pupil	$363	$237	$381	$216
State Revenue per Pupil	$2,737	$990	$2,542	$756
Demographics of District				
Median Family Income	$30,967	$10,671	$33,053	$9,392
% College Educated	13.13	7.49	14.16	6.23
% of Population Between 5 & 19	32.52	5.79	30.69	6.56
% of Population 65 and Over	13.84	3.33	12.40	3.85
% of Families Owning Homes	59.67	13.83	56.59	10.29
% African American	10.77	15.09	14.60	13.15
% Hispanic	8.77	12.50	9.60	15.79
% Below Poverty Line	13.14	8.20	10.75	5.46
Rural	0.23	0.42	0.10	0.30
Suburban	0.54	0.50	0.46	0.50
City	0.30	0.46	0.36	0.48
Cost Factors of District				
Total Number of Students	65,927	187,127	42,827	43,347
Consolidated LEA	0.91	0.28	0.94	0.23
High School LEA	0.02	0.13	0.01	0.09
Elementary LEA	0.07	0.25	0.05	0.22
Characteristics of Students				
% Special Education	10.19	4.66	11.22	3.25
% Poor English Speakers	2.26	3.27	1.71	2.20
% from Military Families Living On Base	0.09	0.27	4.19	8.11
% from Military Families Living Off Base	0.36	0.51	7.82	6.86
Sample Size	27,510		731	

incentive to support their local schools. We also argue that districts with a greater share of owner-occupied housing may have a more vested interest in the schools and a more stable population.

these factors into the models of Poterba and Ladd and Murray, we included these demographic factors in explaining school quality, as proxied not only by expenditures per pupil but also by pupil-teacher ratios.[11]

Cost factors are included in the model, in addition to the demographic variables.[12] Some costs vary inherently across LEAs and are beyond the control of the voting population and school board members. For instance, the LEA and its voting population have limited control over the number of special education students, who require substantially more resources (Lankford and Wycoff, 1999).[13] In addition, special education students may affect the variation in pupil-teacher ratios across LEAs because they spend significant time in smaller classes with more individual attention from teachers. Other factors, such as the total number of students, can create economies (diseconomies) of scale that can reduce (increase) expenditures per pupil and make it more difficult to reduce class sizes.[14]   Finally, because high schools typically have smaller classrooms and are more expensive to operate than elementary schools, the model controls for whether the LEA is high school only or consolidated (both high school and elementary) compared with an elementary LEA.[15]

The model also includes variables that measure the share of military students in the LEA that live on base and off base, as well as indica-

---

[11]The models of Poterba (1997) and Ladd and Murray (2000) measure the relationship between different characteristics of the LEA and support for quality education. Therefore, it is appropriate to use these same explanatory variables if families view pupil-teacher ratio as a measure of quality.

[12]Cost factors are not included in Poterba (1997) or Ladd and Murray (2000).

[13]Cullen (1999) argues that at the margin, LEAs respond to incentives when classifying some special education students. She shows that physical disability rates are relatively constant over time but that learning disability rates have increased. She argues that this increase reflects, in part, an LEA response to financial incentives in state funding formulas.

[14]The total number of students can create economies of scale (decreased cost per student) or diseconomies of scale (increased cost per student). In theory, there is an optimal school size in which costs are minimized. More or fewer students than the optimal size will increase costs per student.

[15]High school students are generally more expensive to educate because they require more specialized and skilled teachers and are usually taught in smaller classes, which require more teachers.

tors variable for whether the LEA has no military students. The funding formula rewards the LEA differently for military on-base and off-base children, so changes in these shares will have a differential effect on LEA funding.

Based on the mean values provided in Table 4.1, the military LEAs appear to have a number of attributes associated with higher-quality schools. For instance, military LEAs have families that are more educated with higher incomes, both of which may lead to a greater demand and ability to pay for education. In addition, the military LEAs have a smaller share of elderly and poor population, both of which may lead to greater support or ability to pay for public education. They also have a larger share of student-age population, which could have two conflicting effects. On the one hand, public support for education will be greater, since more voters have children in school. On the other hand, the cost of raising per pupil expenditures is greater, since most taxpayers are parents, and the costs cannot be spread across many nonparents. The higher the price for increased expenditures per pupil, the lower the demand for raising expenditures or lower pupil-teacher ratios.

Cost factors may also affect expenditures per pupil or reduce the ability of LEAs to reduce their pupil-teacher ratios. For instance, a larger number of students within the nonmilitary LEAs may actually lead to diseconomies of scale and higher costs. However, the non-military LEAs have about the same amount of educationally disadvantaged students, with only slightly lower percentages of special education and slightly higher percentages of students who do not speak English well. The slightly lower number of special education students may create lower costs for the nonmilitary LEAs while the slightly larger number of students who do not speak English well will increase costs. Finally, nonmilitary and military LEAs have about the same number of high school only LEAs, but the military LEAs have more consolidated LEAs and fewer elementary LEAs. The slightly lower number of elementary LEAs may increase their costs relative to other LEAs.

The regression models isolate the effect of military children on resourcing decisions, after controlling for the other demographic and cost characteristics of the LEAs. Military-related students may strain resources in two ways. First, if the military presence limits the local tax base, then the LEA may be resource poor. Second, local taxpayers may be reluctant to accept educational spending increases (and corresponding tax increases) if many of the beneficiaries of those increases are military children with a transient link to the local community. An important measure of the success of Impact Aid funding is its ability to mitigate these two effects so that LEA resourcing patterns are not distorted by the presence and share of military children in the district. The results of the analysis are presented in the next section.

Results

Tables 4.2 and 4.3 display the results of the expenditure-per-pupil and pupil-teacher ratio models. The variables reflect shares of the population with indicator variables for LEAs where the share is zero. For example, the model controls for the share of LEA residents that own their homes and has an indicator variable for whether no residents of the LEA owned their homes. The indicator variable is included to provide extra flexibility for the model and allow the factor to have some discontinuous effect when the share is zero. As a reminder, the regression models adjust for fixed state and time effects while weighting each LEA by the district enrollment.[16]

In both models, the estimates for the control variables are generally consistent with the existing literature or consistent with our expectations. For example, LEA expenditures are positively associated with the median family income and the percentage of the population with a college education. Similarly, LEAs with more special education students have higher spending rates, because their educational costs are above average. As expected, the pattern of significance is similar in the expenditure-per-pupil and pupil-teacher equations, but the signs of the coefficients are opposite. For instance, special education is associated with lower pupil-teacher ratios and higher expenditures per pupil.

The results show that resource use is not sensitive to the percentage of military children living on base, but resource use declines with

---

[16]By weighting observations by enrollment size, the estimates are not distorted by small LEAs.

increases in the percentage of military children living off base.[17] Table 4.2 provides the estimated relationship between different military shares and expenditures per pupil while controlling for non-LEA sources of revenue, the demographics of the districts, and cost factors including the characteristics of the students. The table shows that the percentage of military children living on base has an insignificant effect on expenditure per pupil. This suggests that the Impact Aid funding formula is providing sufficient funding to offset the local education costs of the on-base students.

In contrast, the results for off-base students suggest that these students are straining either the resource base of the districts or the willingness of local taxpayers to finance more educational spending.[18] Expenditures per pupil fall with the percentage of LEA stu-

---

[17]The specifications reported in Tables 4.2 and 4.3 do not account for the percentages of other Impact Aid students in the school district. We report this parsimonious specification here because our emphasis is on the effect of military children on district resources. In other specifications, we also controlled for the percentage of district students who lived on Indian lands, lived in low-rent housing, and were the children of federal employees. These results indicated similar coefficients for military on- and off-base students to those reported in the text. Resource use rose significantly with the share of Indian children in the district but fell as the share of federal employees rose. There was no significant relationship between the share of children in low-rent housing and district resources measures (per pupil expenditures and pupil-teacher ratio).

Our study focused on military students, and we have not fully explored the resource patterns for the other Impact Aid categories. For example, we have not specifically studied districts with a large proportion of Indian children, so we are unfamiliar with unique educational challenges facing these districts or other sources of funding for these districts.

[18]A possible factor confounding the estimates is the endogeneity of the military presence in an LEA. For example, parents may choose to live in an LEA that is remote from the military base, because the LEA has relatively high expenditure per pupil or low pupil-teacher ratio. We tested for this endogeneity in supplemental specifications and found that it was not a problem for our estimates.

The endogeneity issue was potentially important for off-base children but not for on-base children. The stock of military housing is stable and fully occupied at all locations (Buddin et al., 1999). The parents in on-base housing send their children to base schools run by the local school district, so the percentage of on-base children is exogeneous. We did a specification test for the endogeneity of the variable indicating the percentage of off-base students (Hausman, 1978). A reduced-form regression was estimated that included other variables in the model as well as information on the distance between the LEA and a military base and the size of the military population within 40 miles of the LEA. The results indicated that the regressor for the percentage of off-base children and the regression residual were uncorrelated, so the reported regression parameters are consistent and efficient.

dents who are off-base military children. Districts with off-base military children spend systematically less per student than other districts with comparable populations, wealth, and costs. They spend increasingly less as the share of off-base military children increases. More specifically, the estimated elasticity of –0.0301 indicates that for every 1 percent increase in military students who live off base, the expenditures per pupil will decrease by 0.0301 percent.

The effect of military shares on pupil-teacher ratios is reported in Table 4.2. The results parallel those in the expenditure per pupil model. There is no statistically significant relationship between the

Table 4.2

Regression for Factors Affecting LEA Expenditures per Pupil

	Coefficient	Standard Error
Other Sources of District Revenue		
Federal Revenue per Pupil	0.1202*	0.0071
State Revenue per Pupil	0.0335*	0.0107
Demographics of District		
Median Family Income	0.1439*	0.0271
% of Population Between 5 & 19	–0.1171*	0.0171
Indicates No children 5–19	–0.1348	0.0920
% of Population 65 and Over	0.0101	0.0098
% of Families Owning Homes	0.0335	0.0274
Indicates No Families Owning Home	–0.1180	0.1793
% of Families with College Education	0.1156*	0.0094
Indicates No Families with College Education	0.3378*	0.0664
% African American	0.0248*	0.0040
Indicates No African Americans	0.0353*	0.0074
% Hispanic	0.0253*	0.0061
Indicates No Hispanics	0.0252*	0.0080
% Below Poverty Line	–0.0133	0.0110
Indicates No Families Below Poverty Line	–0.0026	0.0861
Rural	–0.0335*	0.0121
Suburban	–0.0128	0.0083
Cost Factors of District		
School Year 1995–1996	0.0289*	0.0042
Total Number of Students	–0.0393*	0.0072
Consolidated LEA	0.0437*	0.0124
High School LEA	0.2713*	0.0131

Table 4.2—continued

	Coefficient	Standard Error
Characteristics of Students		
% Special Education	0.0396*	0.0075
Indicates No Special Education	0.0895*	0.0169
% Poor English Speakers	0.0360*	0.0101
Indicates No Language Problem	0.0119	0.0140
% from Military Families Living On Base	–0.0079	0.0094
Indicates No Military On-Base Students	0.0014	0.0202
% from Military Families Living Off Base	–0.0301*	0.0068
Indicates No Military Off-Base Students	–0.0089	0.0093
Regression Constant	6.2557*	0.2623

NOTE: The dependent variable and independent variables are in natural logarithms except for indicator variables. Data are from 1994–1995 and 1995–1996 school years. Model adjusts for state-level fixed effects and repeated annual observations. The number of observations is 25,410, and adjusted R-squared is 0.7624. Starred entries are significant at 5 percent confidence level.

percentage of military children on base and the LEA's pupil-teacher ratio. LEAs with on-base military children have the same pupil-teacher ratios as nonmilitary LEAs with comparable population, wealth, and cost structures. In contrast, a positive relationship exists

Table 4.3

**Regressions for Factors Affecting LEA
Pupil-Teacher Ratio**

	Coefficient	Standard Error
Other Sources of District Revenue		
Federal Revenue per Pupil	0.0472*	0.0044
State Revenue per Pupil	–0.0286*	0.0051
Demographics of District		
Median Family Income	–0.0249	0.0146
% of Population Between 5 & 19	0.0542*	0.0111
Indicates No children 5–19	0.1815*	0.0600
% of Population 65 and Over	–0.0074	0.0082
% of Families Owning Homes	0.0058	0.0109
Indicates No Families Owning Home	0.1632	0.1038
% of Families with College Education	–0.0646*	0.0060
Indicates No Families with College Education	–0.1188*	0.0596

Table 4.3—continued

	Coeffi- cient	Standard Error
% African American	−0.0056*	0.0019
Indicates No African Americans	−0.0403*	0.0041
% Hispanic	0.0049	0.0033
Indicates No Hispanics	−0.0439*	0.0072
% Below Poverty Line	−0.0015	0.0072
Indicates No Families Below Poverty Line	−0.0779	0.0830
Rural	0.0147*	0.0061
Suburban	0.0234*	0.0053
Cost Factors of District		
School Year 1995–1996	0.0007	0.0022
Total Number of Students	0.0461*	0.0027
Consolidated LEA	−0.0325*	0.0058
High School LEA	−0.0345*	0.0100
Characteristics of Students		
% Special Education	−0.0353*	0.0049
Indicates No Special Education	−0.0578*	0.0103
% Poor English Speakers	−0.0185	0.0049
Indicates No Language Problem	−0.0013	0.0050
% from Military Families Living On Base	0.0015	0.0054
Indicates No Military On-Base Students	0.0056	0.0060
% from Military Families Living Off Base	0.0093*	0.0042
Indicates No Military Off-Base Students	0.0056	0.0060
Regression Constant	3.2873*	0.1720

NOTE: The dependent variable and independent variables are in natural logarithms except for indicator variables. Data are from 1994–1995 and 1995–1996 school years. Model adjusts for state-level fixed effects and repeated annual observations. The number of observations is 25,410, and adjusted R-squared is 0.7624. Starred entries are significant at 5 percent confidence level.

between military students living off base and pupil-teacher ratios. More specifically, the estimated elasticity of 0.0093 for the share of military students living off base indicates that for every 1 percent increase in share of military students in an LEA, the pupil-teacher ratio will increase by 0.0093 percent.

To clarify the implications of the two elasticities, Figures 4.1 and 4.2 demonstrate the relationship between different shares of military students and expenditures per pupil and pupil-teacher ratios. In Figure 4.1, the graph shows that as the share of military students increases, the amount the school districts will spend per pupil declines. For instance, an increase of a 10 percent share of military students will decrease the expenditure per pupil from $5,600 to a little under $5,300. In Figure 4.2, the graph indicates that as the share of military students increases, the pupil-teacher ratios will also increase. Together, these figures suggest that substantial changes in shares of military students within an LEA can affect the expenditures per pupil and pupil-teacher ratios.

Large percentages of off-base children do distort LEA resourcing patterns, but it is unclear what the implications of these distortions are for the military or civilian children in these districts. As discussed above, the connection between the two resource measures (expenditures per pupil and pupil-teacher ratios) and school quality is not strong. The distortions in expenditure rates and pupil-teacher ratios might not be sufficient to translate into changes in student achievement.

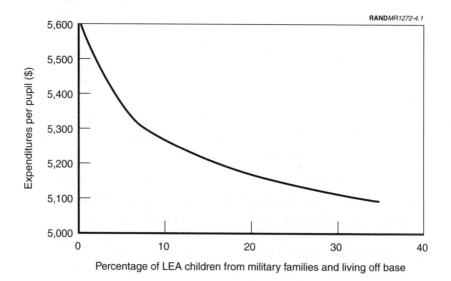

Figure 4.1—Relationship Between Percentage of Children from Military
Families Living Off Base and Expenditures per Pupil

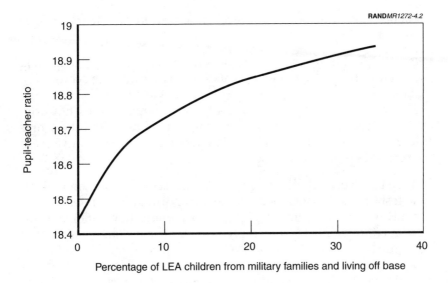

Figure 4.2—Relationship Between Percentage of Children from Military
Families Living Off Base and Pupil-Teacher Ratio

TEST SCORE COMPARISON

A common method for assessing school quality is to compare test
scores across schools or school districts. The problem with this
approach is that test scores intertwine "quality" of the school or
school district with family background factors that have an important bearing on student achievement (Grissmer et al., 1994). For
example, students in a high-income area might have higher test
scores than in a poorer area, but the results might say little about the
"success" of the different schools. Students from higher-income
families may have better access to learning materials from an early
age, and this inherent advantage may help their test scores even if
the school quality is low. In this case, high test scores may provide a
misleading estimate of how successfully a school fosters learning,
because the scores do not recognize that students were not all start-
ing with the same background. A more appropriate measure of
quality would assess whether students of comparable background

reached higher achievement levels in a year in one district versus another.

Another peril in test score comparisons is that the comparisons do not reflect the full set of experiences that enter into the scores. For example, a fourth grade reading score could be low because the quality of the current class or school is low. In many cases, however, many of the students have migrated into the school, and the scores reflect the cumulative reading skill acquired over several years in several different classes or schools.

These test score problems could be addressed with data on individual test scores that included systematic information on the student's family background and schooling history (Hanushek, 1986). Ideally, the data would include a measure of student achievement at the start and the finish of each year as well as measures of school inputs (e.g., class size, expenditures, teacher experience). This type of evidence would clarify which schools were generating the most "value added" or the highest improvement in student achievement.

The knowledge base for military and civilian parents is considerably less than the ideal. First, there is no common test from place to place, so it is hard to compare school systems. Even within states, the testing regimen has changed in several states, so intertemporal comparisons are also difficult. Second, test scores are reported without any controls for student background or migration patterns. In this situation, score differences are a poor indication of the learning opportunities in different schools or LEAs.

These weaknesses notwithstanding, parents are generally willing to place great stock in test scores. In this chapter, we compare test scores in military-impacted LEAs with scores in other parts of the state. The analysis compares the quality of LEAs available to military children (as measured by test scores) and the quality afforded the typical student in other LEAs in the state. The focus on in-state comparisons reflects the lack of a national data set that includes all LEAs and the absence of a consistent measure of student achievement.[19] In other words, while there are test score measures in every

---

[19]There are nationwide data sets produced by the Department of Education. However, these do not include a measure for student achievement. In addition, there are

state, these test score outcomes are not comparable. Scoring in the 60th percentile on a California test and 80 percent of students passing a certain educational proficiency in Texas are not comparable and thus, no consistent measure of performance across all states exists.

The analysis focuses on six states (California, Florida, Maryland, Texas, Virginia, and Washington) that contain 52 percent of all military enrollments.[20] Two sets of results are reported for each state. The first approach looks at differences in unconditional scores, while the second controls for the family background characteristics and socioeconomic status (SES) of the LEA.[21] Unconditional scores give a parent an approximation of how well the district *and its students* compare with others in the state.[22] The scores conditioned on SES provide an adjustment for the background of students in the LEA and offer a better indication of LEA "quality" and success.[23]

In California, all LEAs administer the Stanford Achievement Test, Version 9 (Stanford-9), as a component of the state's STAR

---

national data sets, such as the National Assessment for Education Progress (NAEP) data, that include test scores but do not include all LEAs. Rather, these data sets include only a representative sample of LEAs for each state. Because the Impact Aid program is concentrated in select areas affected by federal activity, the surveyed LEAs may not necessarily overlap with the LEAs that are part of the Impact Aid program.

[20]The test score analysis considers an LEA to be military-related if the district has at least 400 military enrollments. This threshold excludes LEAs with small military enrollments, but it focuses the attention on LEAs serving major military installations. In each state, more than 90 percent of military children covered by Impact Aid are in districts with more than 400 military enrollments.

We explored the sensitivity of our test score results to changing the definition of a military-related district. We tried both a lower cutoff off 200 military-related enrollments and a higher cutoff of 600 military-related enrollments. The results were similar to those reported in the text.

[21]Individual test score data is not available, so the analysis controls for average family background and SES characteristics of the LEA. The controls are median family income, percentage of homes that are owner-occupied, percentage of population with a college degree, percentage of population who are African-American, and percentage of population who are Hispanic.

[22]The unconditional scores would be useful to parents if peer effects were strong. In this case, the parent could match their child with high achievers, and the effect would "rub off" on their child.

[23]The military population is disproportionately young, so few members have teenage children. As a result, the analysis focuses on elementary school test scores.

(Standardized Testing and Reporting) program. Stanford-9 results are based on a national percentile ranking that permits an individual score to be compared to national averages. In other words, a score above the 50th percentile suggests that the individual school is performing above the national average. Figure 4.3 highlights the 1998 reading and math performance of California LEAs with at least 400 military students relative to the state and national averages for fourth graders.

The figure shows that the reading and math test scores in LEAs with military children are 7 and 4 percent lower than in other LEAs. This gap does not necessarily imply that military students are scoring poorly on the tests, however, because military students are typically a small share of enrollments. The poor showing of the military-impacted LEAs is largely a reflection of the SES characteristics of the LEAs near military bases. When the scores are adjusted for SES status of the LEAs, the scores of military-impacted LEAs are slightly better than those of other LEAs in California, but the differences are not

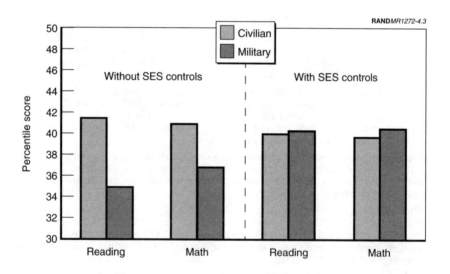

Figure 4.3—California Test Score Comparison for LEAs With and Without Military Children

statistically different from zero.[24] The test scores for both groups of LEAs are 6 or 7 percentage points below the national norms, however.

In Florida, a test referred to as Florida Comprehensive Assessment Test (FCAT) is administered by each LEA. While the FCAT allows comparison within Florida, it is not constructed in a way that allows comparisons to the rest of the nation. Figure 4.4 compares the 1999 weighted-average test score for fourth grade students of the military LEAs with the average score of the state.

The Florida results show that the military-impacted LEAs have substantially higher scores than other districts in the state. The unconditional score is 22 percentile points higher in military-impacted LEAs than in other LEAs. The gap falls substantially when the scores

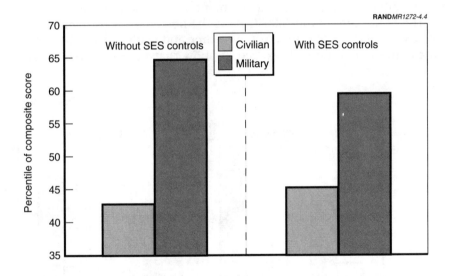

Figure 4.4—Florida Test Score Comparison for LEAs With and Without Military Children

---

[24]The pairwise differences in the figure are all statistically significant at the 5 percent confidence level. In the text below, the differences are also significant unless noted in the text.

are adjusted for SES, but the military districts still enjoy a 13 percent-age point advantage. In Florida, the LEAs are countywide, so the percentage of military children in an LEA is small. As a result, it seems unlikely that high scores by military children would be suffi-cient to account for the gaps in Figure 4.4.

The Maryland results in Figure 4.5 are based on the 1999 Maryland Schools Performance Assessment Program (MSPAP) at the fifth grade levels. The test scores in military-related LEAs are also much higher than in the rest of the state. The percentage scoring satisfactory on the test are 8 and 10 percentage points higher in reading and math, respectively, for districts serving military installations than for other districts. The military-related districts are still above the others after controlling for SES, but the gaps have declined substantially.

Schools in Texas administer the Texas Assessment of Academic Skills (TAAS), which includes an assessment in reading and mathematics. The LEA score on the 1999 TAAS is the percentage of students who pass the basic proficiency test in reading and mathematics. In Figure 4.6, the unconditional test scores show that the military LEAs are

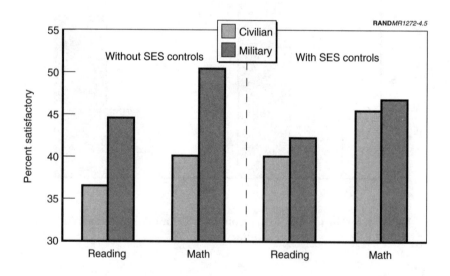

Figure 4.5—Maryland Test Score Comparison for LEAs With and Without Military Children

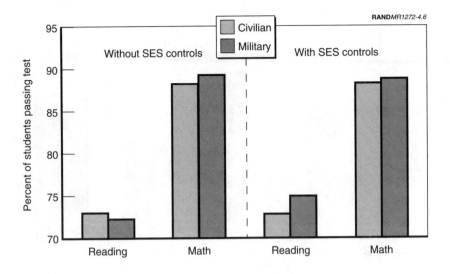

Figure 4.6—Texas Test Score Comparison for LEAs With and Without
Military Children

slightly behind the civilian LEAs in reading and slightly ahead in math. After adjusting for SES, the reading and math pass rates of the military LEAs are significantly above those districts without military installations.

The Virginia test scores (like those in California) are based on the Stanford-9 test, so the scores are comparable with a national sample of fourth graders. In Figure 4.7, the 1999 unconditional scores show that the LEAs with military students are doing very well compared to other schools in Virginia and in the nation. In Virginia, unconditional reading and math scores are 5 percentage points higher in military-related than in other LEAs. This gap largely reflects SES differences between the districts, however, and the rates become statistically insignificant with SES controls.

In Washington state, the math and reading test scores for districts with a military installation are comparable with those for other LEAs. The Washington Assessment of Student Learning (WASL) results are based on 1999 fourth grade assessments. The unconditional test

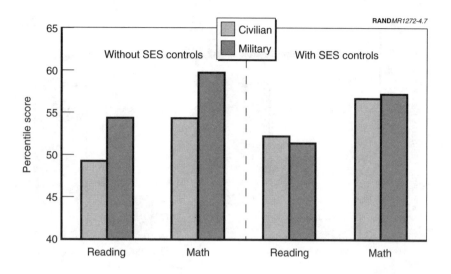

Figure 4.7—Virginia Test Score Comparison for LEAs With and Without Military Children

scores for military-related LEAs are slightly below those of other LEAs, as shown in Figure 4.8, but these differences are not statistically significantly different from zero. The gaps are smaller and still insignificant after controlling for SES.

Taken as a whole, the results suggest that the quality of schools available to military children is generally comparable or above the quality of other schools in the same state. The test scores without adjustments for SES show that military-related LEAs are below average in California, not significantly different from the average in Washington, and above average in Florida, Maryland, and Virginia. The military-related districts in Texas are above average in math and below in reading. SES adjustments separate out some of the effects of family background and provide a more accurate measure of school performance. The adjusted scores show that the military LEAs are above average in Florida, Maryland, and Texas. The scores are not significantly different from the average in California, Virginia, and Washington.

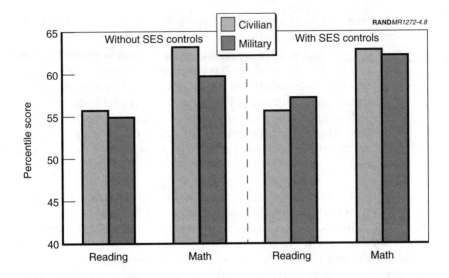

Figure 4.8—Washington State Test Score Comparison for LEAs With and Without Military Children

SUMMARY

This chapter examined resource use (expenditures per pupil and pupil-teacher ratios) and school "quality" (test scores) in LEAs with and without military students.

The resource analysis examined whether the presence or share of military students strains local schooling effort and creates a "burden" for LEAs. Resource use is analyzed with a multivariate model that controls for a variety of funding sources, demographic factors, and costs that affect LEAs. The model allows us to isolate the effects of military-related students on resource use.

- **On-base military students.** The results show that expenditures per pupil and pupil-teacher ratios do not vary significantly with the district's share of on-base military children. The Impact Aid program reimburses enough of the schooling costs for these children to ease any possible burden on the LEAs.

- **Off-base military students**. Expenditures per pupil fall with increases in the district's share of off-base military children. A corresponding increase in pupil-teacher ratio is related to an increase in the share of off-base military children. The result suggests that these students are straining LEA resources. This strain may affect the quality of education available to military and civilian children in districts with a sizable share of off-base students. The magnitude of the resource squeeze is small, however, so the effect on school quality may be modest or inconsequential.

Test scores are used to compare the "quality" of schooling available in military-related LEAs with other LEAs. The goal is to assess whether military children have access to high-quality public schools. The available data are aggregate district-level test scores, so we were unable to control for such factors as family background that may distort the test score patterns. The results suggest that military-related LEAs generally have test scores at or above those for other districts in the state.

Chapter Five

EXTRA COSTS OF EDUCATING MILITARY CHILDREN

Military enrollments may disproportionately alter LEA costs because of unique characteristics of the military population. Military children may not be just additional students that require an "average" increase in expenditures per pupil. Rather, military students may require substantially more or less expenditures than the typical student. A fully funded Impact Aid law would defray the local share of costs for "average" students, but the program would leave a shortfall or surplus if military students cost substantially more or less than average.

Impact Aid funding has been predicated on the reduction of tax base in areas with substantial numbers of federally connected students, but extra costs of military students could provide an additional rationale for LEA funding. For example, frequent relocation of military members is endemic to the military mission. If the transient nature of students imposes substantial costs on LEAs, then it may be more appropriate to spread these extra costs across a broader taxpayer base that benefits from the military mission. Without outside funding, these extra costs might create financial pressures on LEAs to curtail their general instructional program.

This chapter reviews several factors that LEAs consider unusual about military enrollments (Helmick and Hudson, 1997): the mobility or transience of students, enrollment variability, preponderance of low-income students eligible for free/reduced-price school lunch, and special education students. The chapter also considers whether military students might be "above-average" students who have fewer academic problems than the typical student.

STUDENT MOBILITY

High mobility rates for military families mean that military children move from district to district. LEAs argue that these moves create extra costs for diagnostic testing and counseling services (Helmick and Hudson, 1997). Mobility may also have substantial costs for the military students, because curriculum and the pace of learning vary considerably from place to place.

The education literature provides little on how mobility affects students or school district costs. Some studies have shown that mobile students have academic problems. A recent study (Tucker, Marx, and Long, 1998) of 7- to 12-year-old students shows that these problems are isolated in students from nonintact husband/wife households and that students from intact husband/wife households suffer no ill effects from mobility. No data exist on what services schools or school districts provide for relocating students, so it is impossible to assess the costs of these services.

The mobility rates of military and civilian students can be compared using data from the Current Population Survey (CPS). Figure 5.1 shows the percentage of military and civilian students changing counties in the past year.[1] Because few LEAs cross county lines, these intercounty moves should correspond with students changing school district. The rate of military migration is about three times that for civilian students.

Some type of Impact Aid payment might be appropriate to defray extra costs from the high migration rate of military children. There is no systematic evidence, however, of the special services provided to these children or the costs (and effectiveness) of these services.

Even if such evidence existed, the current Impact Aid program is not the ideal vehicle for dealing with these extra costs. First, the funding formula would skew any additional funding toward heavy concentrations of federally connected students. This approach would not

_____

[1]The figure uses data from the March 1998 and March 1999 CPS. This gap between military and civilian mobility rates remains even after adjusting for household status, age and education of household head, and size of urban area.

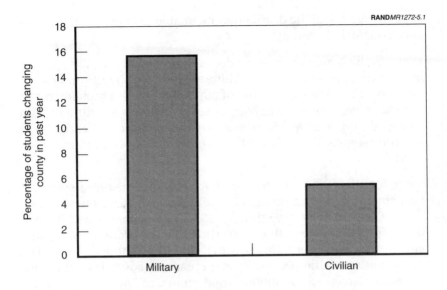

Figure 5.1—Percentage of Military and Civilian Students Moving Between
Counties in the Past Year

be very effective in helping LEAs offset the costs of military migration, which are related to the number of military children and not
their share of enrollment. Second, Impact Aid money is contributed
to the district general fund and is not tied to any specific expenditure. If funding were aimed at the costs of student mobility for military children, then the funding mechanism should be adjusted to a
categorical formula that required LEAs to spend the money on specific, well-defined programs.

ENROLLMENT VARIABILITY

Many LEAs argue that military enrollments are more volatile than
civilian enrollments, so the presence of military children makes it
more difficult to predict enrollments from year to year. School district budgets are based on projected enrollments, and therefore extra
variability strains district resources. If enrollments are higher than
projected, then the district has extra expenses for staff and facilities.
If enrollments are lower than expected, then the district revenue
from state funding is reduced (state funding is typically on a per-

student basis), and the district may be unable to reduce staff because of contractual obligations.

However, high military mobility does not necessarily require changes in military enrollment rates. Military families rotate from base to base over time, but the number of families and military children at a base may vary little from year to year. Military enrollments did change during the base closures and realignments of the early 1990s, but these types of enrollment swings have not occurred in recent years.[2]

Table 5.1 shows the effects of military enrollments on the year-to-year change in LEA enrollments. The results are based on data from the CCD for the 1994–1995 through 1997–1998 school years. The evidence is inconsistent with the assertion that the presence of military students increases enrollment variability in a school district. The first equation is a simple specification that only controls for the presence and percentage of military children in an LEA. There is no tendency for districts with military children to have more enrollment variability than districts without military children. Also, enrollment variability does not increase with the share of military children in the LEA. The second equation expands the enrollment variability model to adjust for various economic, demographic, and district factors that might affect enrollment rates. Again, the military variables are insignificant. Little of the year-to-year variance in enrollment rate is explained by the factors in the model: Enrollments have high variability in LEAs with fewer than 200 students and below-average variability in LEAs with a high percentage of African-American students.

FREE/REDUCED-PRICE SCHOOL LUNCH

Another assertion from LEAs is that military children are predominantly from low-income families as evidenced by their eligibility for the free or reduced-price school lunch program. This Department of Agriculture program offers free school lunches to children from

---

[2]The Impact Aid program was modified in the early 1990s to help LEAs cope with the financial pressures from base closures and realignment.

Table 5.1

Regression for Factors Affecting Percentage Change in LEA Enrollment (Dependent Variable Measure in Logs)

Variable	Military Presence Only		Full Specification	
	Coeffi-cient	Standard Error	Coeffi-cient	Standard Error
% from Military Students	−0.0840	0.5981	0.1569	0.5334
Indicates No Military Students	0.0197	0.0884	0.0594	0.0687
LEA Has Fewer Than 200 students			0.6327*	0.1013
Log of Number of Students			0.0343	0.0349
Median Family Income			0.0101	0.0052
% Below Poverty Line			−0.0002	0.0041
% of Families with College Education			−0.0054	0.0028
% of Families Owning Home			−0.0058	0.0034
% Poor English Speakers			0.0246	0.0225
% African-American			−0.0045*	0.0021
% Hispanic			0.0000	0.0034
Consolidated LEA			0.0822	0.0665
High School LEA			0.0794	0.1115
Rural Area			0.1139	0.0857
Suburban Area			−0.0167	0.0722
Regression Constant	−0.9415*	0.0864	−1.2474*	0.3123

NOTE: Standard errors have been adjusted for the presence of multiple observations for each LEA. The omitted reference categories are elementary school LEAs (versus consolidated or high school) and urban area (versus rural or suburban areas). Starred entries are significant at 5 percent confidence level.

households with incomes less than or equal to 130 percent of the federal poverty guidelines and reduced-price meals to children from households with incomes at or below 185 percent of the guidelines. The poverty guidelines are a function of household size.

The evidence suggests that a sizable percentage of military-related children do receive free/reduced-price school lunch, but the percentage is substantially below that for civilian children. The CPS collected information on program participation. Figure 5.2 shows that 42 percent of civilian children participate in the lunch program compared with 29 percent of military children. The main reason for

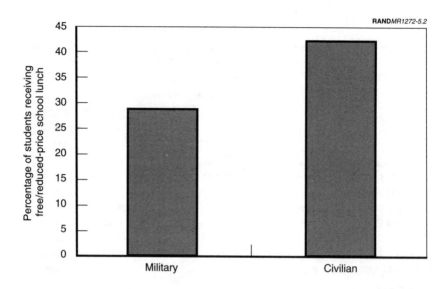

Figure 5.2—Percentage of Military and Civilian Children Receiving Free or Reduced-Price School Lunches

the gap between military and civilian children is that single-parent families are underrepresented in the military population.[3] If the percentages are adjusted for differences in age, demographics, and family structure in the two groups, the lunch participation rates are comparable between military and civilian children.

The high proportion of military families earning less than 185 percent of the poverty guidelines reflects the unique military compensation package. Unlike civilian compensation, military compensation includes housing benefits for military families. These families either receive a nontaxable housing allowance for civilian sector housing or rent-free housing on base. Lunch program eligibility does not count the in-kind value of on-base housing or the tax benefit of the housing allowance toward determining family income. Because young families typically spend 20 to 30 percent of their income on housing (Buddin et al., 1999), many military families are nominally

---

[3]The poverty rate for female-headed families is more than five times that for all other families (Sawhill, 1988).

eligible for the lunch program, when their "true" income (including the value of the housing benefit) is beyond the federal guidelines.[4] As a result, military families eligible for the lunch program have substantially more family wealth than their civilian counterparts.

Participation rates in the free/reduced-price lunch program are important because these rates trigger funding under the massive Title I program of the Department of Education. Title I provides $8 billion annually to fund local school programs targeted toward low-income children. Military children in the school lunch program make the LEA eligible for Title I funding in addition to the Impact Aid funding. Because military families have greater "true" incomes than their civilian counterparts, the extra Title I funding may overcompensate for programs aimed at many of these military children.

Evidence from DoD Domestic Dependents Elementary and Secondary Schools (DDESS) is consistent with our conjecture that the military children receiving free/reduced-price lunches have fewer academic problems than their civilian counterparts. Ballator and Jerry (1999) analyzed the test scores of military children in DoD schools. They found that military children receiving free/reduced-price school lunch performed significantly better than a national sample of nonmilitary children participating in the program.

ABOVE-AVERAGE STUDENTS

A circumstantial case suggests that military children may be above-average students and require less education resources than the typical student. The evidence is fragmentary, because test score information is typically aggregated across military and civilian children. Nonetheless, an interesting picture does emerge from evidence about the family backgrounds of military children as well as the performance of military children in districts that consist only of military children.[5]

---

[4]Food stamp eligibility for military families is also distorted by the way that military housing benefits are counted (or not counted) in assessing family income (Pleeter, 1996).

[5]An interesting approach to comparing the academic skills of military and civilian children would be to compare the test scores of military children in on-base public schools with the tests scores of similar civilian children in the same school district.

Family Background

Military families have backgrounds that suggest that their children will do well in school. Military members are screened for admission into the military, and the quality of the force has been very high for the past several years. Nearly all enlistees were high school graduates or better before joining, and 75 percent scored above the national mean on the military's achievement test.[6] Also, nearly 90 percent of military school-age children reside in an intact husband/wife family compared with 70 percent of civilian school-age children.

These types of background characteristics suggest that the typical military students might inherently do better than their civilian counterparts. Numerous studies have shown the importance of parental education and family structure on student achievement (Grissmer et al., 1994; Tucker, Marx, and Long, 1998). Because the military has few dropouts and few single-parent families, military students would (on average) be expected to do well in school.

Public Districts with Nearly All Military Students

In most cases, public school test scores are not reported separately for military and civilian students, so it is impossible to compare the achievement levels of these two groups of students. However, seven public school districts consisting almost entirely of military children can be compared to other districts. In these cases, the district score indicates how well the military students are doing.

Test scores reflect the family background of the student as well as their cumulative classroom experience. Because military students have high mobility rates, their scores may have little to do with the quality of their current school. Rather, high test scores for military

---

Unfortunately, there is no systematic listing of on-base schools, so this type of intra-district comparison is not possible. As a result, our analysis focused on districtwide comparisons.

[6]Military applicants take the Armed Services Vocational Aptitude Battery (ASVAB) to determine their eligibility for enlistment. Composite scores from the ASVAB are used to construct an Armed Forces Qualification Test (AFQT) percentile. These percentile rankings are tied to a national sample of youth.

children reflect both the quality of their schooling and their family background.

At Minot AFB and Grand Forks AFB, North Dakota does not report separate district test scores for the base districts. The scores from these students seem to be averaged in with those from the Minot and Grand Forks school districts. These districts' scores are quite similar to the state average, but it is impossible to disentangle the military scores from the district average.

The military students at the Fort Huachuca Accommodation Schools do well compared to the typical Arizona student. The fourth-, fifth-, and sixth-grade reading scores are in the 66th, 64th, and 68th percentile, respectively, of the nationally referenced Stanford-9. Similarly, the fourth grade, fifth grade, and sixth grade math scores are in the 53rd, 58th, and 65th percentile of the national population.

The Fort Leavenworth School District has test scores that are substantially above the state averages, but part of this difference probably reflects features unique to the base. The average percentage of correct answers on the reading test was 71.0 at Fort Leavenworth compared with 64.1 for the state as a whole. The math score was 68.9 compared with that state average of 59.7. Fort Leavenworth is an officer training school, so twice as many officers as enlisted personnel are at the base. The high test scores reflect the above-average SES of the officer corps compared with a more general military population.

In Texas, military children in the state's three military districts (Fort Sam Houston, Lackland, and Randolph Field Independent school districts) do well on the state achievement tests. The statewide pass rate in fourth grade reading is 73 percent as compared with 75, 93, and 88 percent at Fort Sam Houston, Lackland, and Randolph, respectively. The statewide pass rate on the fourth grade math test was 88 percent, but military children at Fort Sam Houston, Lackland, and Randolph had pass rates of 98, 93, and 97, respectively.

The evidence from these military-only public schools suggests that military students may be above-average. The evidence is sketchy, however, because these districts represent such a small share of the military population. Individual test score data on military children would be a big help in assessing the "quality" of these students.

Military Students in DoD Schools

DDESS participated in the 1998 NAEP reading assessment. The NAEP is the only nationally representative assessment of student achievement. Ballator and Jerry (1999) have analyzed the DDESS results and compared the performance of these military children with civilian children in the country.

The NAEP provides further evidence that military children are above-average academic achievers. The DDESS students scored significantly higher than the national student population in both fourth and eighth grade reading. The strong performance of these military children might be interpreted as an indication that DDESS is doing a much better job at educating children than the typical public school system. This seems unlikely to explain the test score gap, however, since the mobility at these schools is 30 to 40 percent per year. Two factors are more plausible explanations for the success of military children. First, as discussed above, the family background of military families suggests that these students would be above-average achievers. Second, because many of the DDESS students are new to the system each year, the test score gap may indicate that the public schools are doing a good job of training these military children.

SPECIAL EDUCATION

Funding of special education has long been a problem for LEAs, irrespective of their funding support under Impact Aid. The Education for All Handicapped Children Act (EHA) was passed by the federal government in 1975 and mandated that students with disabilities were entitled to "free appropriate education." Since the passage of the EHA, the special education share of enrollments has risen from 8 percent to 12 percent. Most of the increase in special education has been in students diagnosed with learning disabilities: These students were 7.5 percent of special education students in 1975 and are 50 percent today (Cullen, 1997).

The costs of special education have become a burden on most school districts. The EHA law created a federal mandate for expanding special education services, but the costs have been largely borne by state and local governments. Expenditures per pupil for special education costs are estimated at 2.3 times those for general education students

(Chaikind, Danielson, and Brauen, 1993). The average LEA budget share devoted to special education has risen from 4 percent in 1975 to 17 percent in recent years (Rothstein and Miles, 1995). The EHA created a federal mandate for expanding special education services, but federal funding has borne only a portion of the costs. Federal programs reimburse LEAs for about 10 percent of special education costs (about the same share of general education costs), so the new costs have been largely borne by state and local governments (Cullen, 1997).

Many military-related LEAs are concerned about the costs of special education for military children (Helmick and Hudson, 1997; Knott, 1995; Beauchamp and McAllister, 1995). The assertion is that funding is insufficient to cover these extra costs and that special education constitutes a larger share of military enrollments than in the general student population.

A military presence increases the number of special education students in nearby LEAs, but the increase is *less* than proportional to the size of the military population. Table 5.2 shows that approximately 11 percent of students in the nation are enrolled in special education. The special education rate in LEAs with military children is about 12 percent, slightly higher than the U.S. average. Within these military-related LEAs, however, special education rates for military children are only about two-thirds those of nonmilitary, civilian children. The table also shows the results of pairwise comparisons of special education rates at each military-related LEA. These results show that the civilian special education rate is significantly more than the military rate in about 50 percent of LEAs.

The Impact Aid law has a special provision that reimburses LEAs for a portion of the costs of special education for military and children living on Indian lands. The special education funding is over and above the funding through BSP. The additional funding is dispersed on a pro rata basis where children of military off-base personnel receive a weight equal to 50 percent of the weight for children of on-base military personnel or those on Indian lands (the Impact Aid law does not provide special education money for the children of federal employees or civilians living in low-rent housing). The special education appropriation is divided amongst LEAs in proportion to their

Table 5.2

Comparisons of Civilian and Military Students in Special Education by School Year (Percentages)

	1994–1995	1995–1996	1996–1997	1997–1998	1998–1999
National	11.2	10.8	11.2	11.9	11.3
Impact Aid LEAs with Military Children					
Civilian Children	12.2	12.4	12.4	13.0	12.5
Military Children	8.0	8.3	8.6	8.7	8.4
LEA-Level Comparisons					
Civilian Exceeds Military Percentage	49.0	51.9	53.1	54.2	51.9
Civilian Same as Military Percentage	41.3	39.0	35.5	36.6	38.3
Military Exceeds Civilian Percentage	9.8	9.1	11.4	9.2	9.8

NOTE: The LEA-Level Comparisons are based on a difference in proportions test that measures whether the civilian proportion of special education in the LEA minus the military share of special education in the LEA is significantly different from zero at the 5 percent confidence level.

weighted federally connected special education population, regardless of the concentration of federally connected special education students. In 1999, the funding was $1,150 for a special education student living on a military base or on Indian lands and $575 for a military child living off base. Unlike the BSP funding, however, the special education money must be spent on special education programs.

An irony of the Impact Aid law is that the special education provision of the law is simple relative to the BSP portion of the law. While BSP varies drastically from place to place, the special education allotment does not vary at all with location. Figure 5.3 illustrates the total LEA allotment for the typical on-base, off-base, and Indian special education student. Compared with the BSP program, the special education allotment is very generous to off-base military children, i.e., the special education payment of $575 is almost nine times as large as the BSP payment of $65.80. Special education and BSP funding are nearly equal for a special education student living on base. The special education funding for an Indian child is only about 40 percent of the funding awarded through BSP.

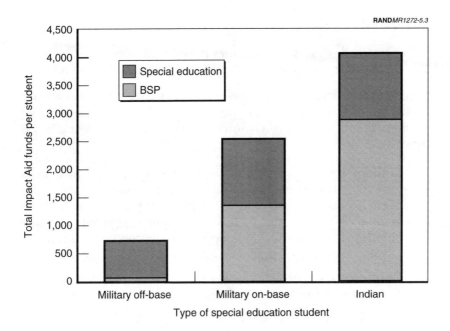

Figure 5.3—Generosity of Impact Aid Program for Special Education
Students for Different Groups of Students

The special education funding under the Impact Aid program is in addition to other state and federal funding for special education. The special education provision of Impact Aid is aimed at replacing the local share of cost for special education. For example, suppose that LEA expenditures per pupil were $6,000 per year. The average cost for a special education student in the district would be $13,800 ($6,000 times 2.3). Because a fully funded Impact Aid program is intended to cover the local share of education costs (50 percent of expenditures), the federal reimbursement for this "typical" special education child would be $6,900 (50 percent of $13,800). Then, the required BSP and special education allotments for an on-base student would be $3,000 and $3,900, respectively. At current funding levels, both payments are well below these targets, therefore the shortfall must be made up with some combination of local, state, and federal funds.

SUMMARY

This chapter has examined whether the education cost for a military child is more or less than that for the typical public school child.

The evidence suggests that these students may pose some extra costs, but these costs might not be large. In other respects, however, military children may have below-average costs, so the net effect is unclear.

- **Student Mobility.** Military students have district-to-district mobility rates three times those of other students. This presumably raises testing and counseling costs for LEAs, but there is no evidence of the extent of the services or magnitude of these charges. Evidence does suggest that migration will not have an adverse affect on the academic performance of military children.

- **Enrollment Variability.** Year-to-year enrollment variability is not related to the presence of military children in an LEA.

- **Free/Reduced-Price School Lunch.** The participation rate of military children is *lower* than that for the civilian children. Many military children are eligible for the lunch program, but this eligibility reflects the unique military compensation package that provides "free" on-base housing.

- **Above-Average Students.** Background characteristics of military parents (e.g., high school graduation status and a preponderance of intact husband/wife households) suggest the children of military members would be above-average students. The test scores of military children in DoD schools and in "military-only" public school systems are consistent with this conjecture.

- **Special Education.** The share of special education students is much lower for the military students than for nonmilitary students. The Impact Aid allotment for special education students is small and insufficient to offset the LEAs' local costs for these students. Other state and federal programs provide additional funding for special education, however, so the effects of the shortfall are unclear.

Chapter Six

CONCLUSIONS

The variance in payments under Impact Aid is too large. The "needs" for different classes of students may differ, but the funding formula creates huge differences in funding for the same type of student. Equity and fairness suggest that the program should move toward an approach that substantially reduces the variance in payments.

The linkage of Impact Aid funding to shares of federally connected students in an LEA is inherently flawed. LEA boundaries are not defined consistently across states, and this inconsistency creates funding inequities under the Impact Aid funding formula. Several states with large military bases have countywide school districts, so the military share of enrollments is small even near large bases. Other states have several LEAs in the same county or city, so a base of comparable size is associated with a large share of military students in nearby LEAs. These historical and political differences in defining LEAs lead to dramatic funding swings under the LOT formula. The Impact Aid reimbursement for an on-base student in Florida is $625 compared with $1,970 in Texas, and the funding gap is driven primarily by the difference between county-level districts in Florida and small districts in Texas. The taxpayers of Florida may be able to makeup this shortfall in funding, but the funding policy punishes them unfairly for the way the state defines LEA boundaries.

The evidence indicates that the education opportunities for military and civilian children are moderately comparable. Test scores in military-related LEAs are generally at or above those of other LEAs in their respective states. Similarly, expenditures per pupil and pupil-teacher ratios vary across districts, but these resources are not strained by the presence of on-base military children. On a less positive note, off-base military students do seem to tax LEA resources, so military children in LEAs with large numbers of military children face below-average expenditures per pupil and above-average pupil-teacher ratios. The differences might not be large enough to affect achievement, but the evidence suggests that the Impact Aid reimbursement for off-base military children could be too low.

The evidence suggests that some LEA concerns about the extra costs of military children may be misplaced. Military presence does not contribute significantly to year-to-year enrollment variability. Limited evidence suggests that military students may be above-average students that might have below-average schooling costs.

Special education rates are not high for the military population, but special education funding is a problem for LEAs. The funding for federally connected students is inherently linked to the broader issue of federal and state support for special education programs. One possible improvement in the federal program might be to integrate the benefit for federally connected students with the broader federal support for special education. This approach would avoid redundancy in measuring these expenditures and monitoring LEA special education programs.

Migration rates are much higher for military children than for civilian children. DoD should evaluate the cost that this migration imposes on military children and local LEAs. If costs are large, DoD could modify military after-school programs to ease these transitions. For example, local teachers could be hired in the late summer to prepare new military arrivals for their new schools.

BIBLIOGRAPHY

Ballator, Nada, and Laura Jerry, *NAEP 1998 Reading Report for the Department of Defense Domestic Dependent Elementary and Secondary Schools*, U.S. Department of Education, NCES 1999-460 DDESS, 1999.

Beadie, Nancy, "The Limits of Standardization and the Importance of Constituencies: Historical Tensions in the Relationship Between State Authority and Local Control," in Neil D. Theobald and Betty Malen, eds., *Balancing Local Control and State Responsibility for K–12 Education*, Larchmont, N.Y.: Eye on Education, 2000.

Beauchamp, Barry, and Vernon McAllister, "Impact Aid and Children of the Military," U.S. House of Representatives, testimony before Subcommittee on Early Childhood, Youth, and Families Hearing on Impact Aid, July 1995.

Buddin, Richard, Carole Roan Gresenz, Susan D. Hosek, Marc N. Elliott, and Jennifer Hawes-Dawson, *An Evaluation of Housing Options for Military Families*, Santa Monica, Calif.: RAND, MR-1020-OSD, 1999.

Card, David, and Alan B. Krueger, "Does School Quality Matter? Return to Education and the Characteristics of Public Schools in the United States," Journal of Political Economy, Vol. 100, No. 1, February 1992, pp. 1–40.

Chaikind, Stephen, Louis C. Danielson, and Marsha L. Brauen, "What Do We Know About the Costs of Special Education? A Selected Review," *Journal of Special Education*, Vol. 26, 1993, pp. 344–370.

Coons, John E., William H. Clune, III, Stephen D. Sugarman, *Private Wealth and Public Education*, Cambridge, Mass.: Harvard University Press, 1970.

Cullen, Julie Berry, "Essays on Special Education Finance and Intergovernmental Relations," Ph.D. dissertation, Massachusetts Institute of Technology, 1997.

Cullen, Julie Berry, "The Impact of Fiscal Incentives on Student Disability Rates," Working Paper 7173, National Bureau of Economic Research, Cambridge, Mass., June 1999.

Dardia, Michael, Kevin F. McCarthy, Jesse D. Malkin, and George Vernez, *The Effects of Military Base Closures on Local Communities: A Short-Term Perspective*, Santa Monica, Calif.: RAND, MR-667-OSD, 1996.

Ehrenberg, Ronald G., and Dominic J. Brewer, "Did Teachers' Verbal Ability and Race Matter in the 1960's? Coleman Revisited," *Economics of Education Review*, Vol. 14, No. 1, 1995, pp 1–23.

Evans, William N., Sheila E. Murray, and Robert M. Schwab, "Towards Increased Centralization in Public School Finance," working paper, University of Maryland, 1996.

Ferguson, Ronald F., "Paying for Public Education: New Evidence on How and Why Money Matters," *Harvard Journal of Legislation*, Vol. 28, No. 2, Summer 1991, pp. 465–498.

Gill, Brian, correspondence with officials at the U.S. Department of Education, 2000a.

Gill, Brian, interviews with officials of the NAFIS and the Department of Education, Washington, D.C., 2000b.

Goldhaber, Dan D., and Dominic J. Brewer, "Why Don't Schools and Teachers Seem to Matter? Assessing the Impact of Unobservables on Educational Productivity," *Journal of Human Resources*, Vol. 32, No. 3, Summer 1997, pp. 505–523.

Goodling, Rep. Bill, Chairman, Committee on Education and the Workforce, "Opening Remarks: The Impact Aid Reauthorization Act of 2000," U.S. House of Representatives, February 16, 2000.

Grissmer, David W., Sheila Nataraj Kirby, Mark Berends, and Stephanie Williamson, *Student Achievement and the Changing American Family*, Santa Monica, Calif.: RAND, MR-488-LE, 1994.

Hanushek, Eric. A., "The Economics of Schooling: Production and Efficiency in Public Schools, *Journal of Economic Literature*, Vol. 24, No. 3, Fall 1986, pp. 1141–1177.

Hausman, Jerry A., "Specification Tests in Econometrics," *Econometrica*, Vol. 46, No. 6, 1978, pp. 1251–1272.

Helmick, John, and Lisa Hudson, *A Study of Schools Serving Military Families in the United States*, Arlington, Va.: Defense Manpower Data Center, 1997.

Houston, Robert, and Eugenia F. Toma, "Home Schooling: An Alternative School Choice," working paper, Eastern Kentucky University and University of Kentucky, 1999.

Knott, Richard J., "Impact Aid and Children of the Military," U.S. House of Representatives, testimony before Subcommittee on Early Childhood, Youth, and Families Hearing on Impact Aid, July 1995.

Krueger, Alan B., and Diane M. Whitmore, "The Effect of Attending a Small Class in the Early Grades on College-Test Taking and Middle School Test Results: Evidence From Project Star," Working Paper 7657, National Bureau of Economic Research, 2000.

Ladd, Helen F., and Sheila E. Murray, "Intergenerational Conflict Reconsidered: County Demographic Structure and the Demand for Public Education," working paper, Duke University, 2000.

Lankford, Hamilton, and James Wycoff, "The Allocation of Resources to Special Education and Regular Instruction in New York State," in Thomas B. Parrish, Jay G. Chambers, and Cassandra M. Guarino, eds., *Funding Special Education*, Thousand Oaks, Calif.: Corwin Press, Inc., 1999.

Military Impacted School Association (MISA), website at http://www.esu3.k12.ne.us/districts/bellevue/misa/misahome.html, 2000.

Murray, Sheila, William N. Evans, and Robert M. Schwab, "Education Finance Reform and the Distribution of Education Resources," *American Economic Review*, Vol. 88, No. 3, 1998, pp. 205–217.

National Association of Federally Impacted Schools (NAFIS) website at http://www.sso.org/nafis/reauthor.htm, 2000.

National Center for Education Statistics (NCES), *School District Data Book*, Volume 95-04, April 1995.

_____, *Digest of Education Statistics*, 1998.

_____, *Common Core Data (CCD) School Years 1993–1994 through 1997–1998*, CD-ROM, 2000.

Pleeter, Saul, "Are Military Housing Allowances Adequate?" paper presented at the Western Economics Association meetings in San Francisco, July 1996.

Poterba, James M., "Demographic Structure and the Political Economy of Public Education," *Journal of Policy Analysis and Management*, Vol. 16, No. 1, Winter 1997, pp. 48–66.

Rothstein, Richard, with Karen Hawley Miles, *Where's the Money Gone? Changes in the Level and Composition of Education Spending*, Washington, D.C.: Economic Policy Institute, 1995.

Sander, William, "Expenditures and Student Achievement in Illinois" *Journal of Public Economics*, Vol. 52, No. 3, October 1993, pp. 403–416.

Sawhill, Isabel V., "Poverty in the U.S.: Why Is It So Persistent?" *Journal of Economic Literature*, Vol. 26, No. 3, September 1988, pp. 1073–1119.

Trejos, Nancy, and Steve Vogel, "Mustering for School at Home," *Washington Post*, April 6, 2000.

Tucker, C. Jack, Jonathan Marx, and Larry Long, "'Moving On': Residential Mobility and Children's School Lives," *Sociology of Education*, Vol. 71, April 1998, pp. 111–129.

U.S. Department of Education, "Biennial Evaluation Report—FY93–94," 1995, Chapter 109.

Wise, Arthur E., *Rich Schools, Poor Schools: The Promise of Equal Educational Opportunity,* Chicago: University of Chicago Press, 1968.